GRANITE
MOUNTAIN

GRANITE MOUNTAIN

The Firsthand Account of a Tragic Wildfire,
Its Lone Survivor, and the Firefighters
Who Made the Ultimate Sacrifice

BRENDAN McDONOUGH

WITH STEPHAN TALTY

hachette
BOOKS

NEW YORK   BOSTON

Copyright © 2016 by Brendan McDonough

Cover design by Amanda Kain
Cover copyright © 2017 by Hachette Book Group, Inc.

Hachette Books
Hachette Book Group
1290 Avenue of the Americas, New York, NY 10104
hachettebooks.com
twitter.com/hachettebooks

Originally published as *My Lost Brothers* in hardcover and ebook by Hachette Books in May 2016.
First mass market media tie-in edition: September 2017

Hachette Books is a division of Hachette Book Group, Inc. The Hachette Books name and logo are trademarks of Hachette Book Group, Inc.

The publisher is not responsible for websites (or their content) that are not owned by the publisher.

The Hachette Speakers Bureau provides a wide range of authors for speaking events. To find out more, go to www.hachettespeakersbureau.com or call (866) 376-6591.

LCCN: 2016015594
ISBN: 978-0-316-51155-1 (mass market)

Printed in the United States of America

OPM

10 9 8 7 6 5 4 3 2 1

To my brothers

PROLOGUE:
GRANITE MOUNTAIN

It was about nine thirty a.m. when we tramped into the station, back from a six-mile run in the hills. The desert was starting to cook and the run had been grueling. We grabbed our water bottles and pulled the gunmetal-gray chairs into a semicircle and just sat there, dazed, chugging water, saying nothing at all.

This was a time when the crew ragged on each other and tried to get someone going. Workingman's theater. The basic horribleness of us all as rookies was a popular subject. Today was my turn.

"Donut," Chris said, looking at me, sweat running down his face, "you remember your first week? You ran like old people fuck. *Slooooooooooowly.*"

Laughter rang off the corrugated roof of the station. I smiled. Hell, it was true.

"Looks like a gazelle, runs like Chris Farley, that's me," I shot back. Never let them know it hurts.

Just then I heard Jesse call out something. "Smoke."

That got all our attention. Smoke? Here in Prescott? We walked outside.

Jesse pointed to Granite Mountain, northwest of us. There it was, on the left-hand shoulder. Light gray, not moving.

"Jesus, not now," someone mumbled. We were drained. A six-mile run in the desert heat will wear you out.

We started getting ready, putting on our yellow long-sleeve Nomex shirts and our Nomex pants and our hand-made leather boots. We were willing the smoke to turn white, which would mean the fire was losing power. But it kept getting darker, bit by bit. It was moving, too, to the east, by the looks of it. Which meant the fire was getting bigger and stronger and it was coming toward us.

We all knew the names of wildfires that hadn't ended well: the Great Hinckley Fire in Minnesota, where a "fire tornado" burned so hot barrels of nails melted, train wheels fused with the steel rails, and 418 people died. Or the 1990 Dude Fire, which turned from a nothing blaze to a thirty-foot wall of flame moving at sixty miles per hour before it chased down and killed a crew of five inmate firefighters and their guard. The Oakland Firestorm, driven by a dry Diablo wind, jumped an eight-lane freeway, burned a house every eleven seconds, and killed twenty-five people. It came close to burning down Oakland itself. Mann Gulch, where a blowup cost thirteen smokejumpers their lives. In Esperanza, it was five firefighters, dead trying to protect a house.

Each one had different causes, different conditions, different terrains. But they all shared one factor: tinderbox dryness in the brush and wood that fueled them. And that sure as hell was true for Prescott, Arizona. It was drought conditions here.

We'd been in towns after the inferno had gone through. They were sad, bitter places, places that had been erased, just like the memories and keepsakes that the fire had claimed. I thought of my two-year-old daughter at home with her mom. What game was she playing right this minute? Was she gazing out the window, watching the smoke approach? I thought of the pictures of her taped to our fridge.

In my two years with Granite Mountain, I'd walked past many homes just like mine, but gutted and seared. The people traumatized, searching for scraps of their former lives. You never get back everything you lose in a fire. It's a bad time. It hurts.

But as much as I'd dreaded this moment, I'd been waiting for it, too. Now I could show my family what I'd been doing for two years, show them I was putting my life on the line to keep them and Prescott safe. One final proof that I wasn't the old Brendan anymore.

The radio began heating up. The whole town—cops, structure firemen, Forestry—was watching the fireline and waiting to see which way the smoke moved. It was turning darker and creeping eastward, ever so slightly. The flames even had a name: the Doce Fire, after a local landmark.

"Let's get ready," Jesse said. "And listen up. Eat now. If we're working Prescott, we sure as shit won't have time to eat lunch."

Peak burning time in the Southwest is from noon to five p.m. Temperatures rise, relative humidity drops, winds pick up. Those five hours are the ones you live for.

We refilled our water canisters, then found our chairs again and sat simmering in the ninety-five-degree heat. We waited and watched the smoke plume.

Dark gray now. We couldn't go until we were called in. And the darker the smoke got, the greater the chance that call would come.

It went to black against the dome of blue sky. Then it started moving to the northeast, faster. The radio crackled. "Crew Seven."

That was us. We started the buggies, big white Ford F-450 trucks with equipment lockers above our heads that held our packs, bins on the side of the trucks that held all our other gear, and captain's chairs for us to sit on during the drive to the fire line. The drivers revved the engines and tore out of the station's driveway.

The adrenaline was just about lifting me out of my seat. "Gonna get some!" I yelled out as we sped off down Sixth Street. "*Woooohoooo!*" Air gusting through the windows, wheels squealing around the corners, headed right at Granite Mountain. It was about twenty minutes to the fire line.

The smoke was moving all the time. We swiveled our heads to keep it in sight as the buggy took corners.

We were driving down a two-lane highway now. As we got close, the houses on the other side of the mountain were being evacuated. They sat abandoned, some with the doors left wide open. Not a soul to be seen. The place was under mandatory evacuation. But that didn't mean everyone was out.

We headed toward a checkpoint with a wooden barrier thrown up across the road; it was there to keep non–emergency personnel from getting near the fire. The guys manning the barrier saw us coming and pulled it back, shouting to each other that we were the last car getting through before the road closed.

They don't close roads unless the fire is moving fast. From that alone, we realized things were heating up. I knew there were people in cars going the other way on the phone with their insurance companies, watching the fire approach and thinking, *My house is gone.*

We switched to an old dirt road that would take us toward the fire line. It was rutted and pitched, and the buggy swung left and right as we drove down it.

Jesse was on the radio trying to get a grip on where we should be. What's the strategy? Who's supervising? Where do we engage? You need to fight a fire from the heel, set an anchor, outflank it, and put it to rest.

But this was Prescott and everyone wanted in. There were cop cars screaming past and fire companies and dudes in white shirts running around yelling into their radios. It was chaos. Jesse was asking people what the plan was and they were telling him: *We're working on it*. The fire was out of control, zero percent contained. Everywhere you looked it was going off.

My heart was revving so high my veins ached. Chris slowed the buggy and as soon as it came to a stop, we jumped out.

The guys were amped. You could feel it. It reminded me of those soldiers at Stalingrad: The fire was threatening *our* homes, *our* families. It was time to fight.

Jesse went off and got the plan of attack before returning to give us a quick briefing. When Jesse left, we grabbed our saws and hucked our packs out of the back as if they were brown-bag lunches and strapped them on. Then we hustled out toward the brush. Chainsaws were going off one after the other, *rawwwrrr-rawwwrrr-RAWWWRRR*. Fifty pounds felt like five. And in the distance, we could see the fire sucking in air.

The blaze was coming down a slope three-quarters of a mile ahead of us. Jesse called out a basic strategy. "For now," he yelled, "it can cross the highway to the north. But we can't let it cross west of the dirt road. Everyone got it?"

Jesse set the anchor—the barrier from which we'd start building the fire line—then pointed out spots for me and Chris to burn. I didn't even have time to put a piece of chaw in my cheek before we were hiking down the highway, looking for a place to go in.

Chris and I found a gap in the brush and he went first. It was half-dark in there. The branches scraped along the nylon of my pack as I ducked to get through, pinging on my helmet. I slotted my sunglasses and grabbed my drip torch, pulling a lighter out of my pocket. A drip torch is a gallon-sized metal can used to burn brush and deprive the wild-fire of fuel. It drips out a 70/30 mix of diesel and gasoline through a wick, which is lit at the end. The burning mixture falls onto the grass or brush or what have you and sets it alight. Crews attach torches to trucks and even helicopters, but mostly it's hotshots out there burning shit up. No time to cry about the lost wildlife, just light it up and keep moving.

I was trying to light the wick with a Bic lighter, but the damn thing wouldn't catch. Chris had his lit and was wait-ing for me, impatience written all over his face.

"Come on, damn it," I said, and flicked the lighter again. Nothing. Once more. The wick lit and I tucked the lighter away. I gripped my Pulaski in my right hand and my drip torch in my left, and Chris and I moved into scrub oak.

As soon as we got past the brush to a small clearing, we saw the fire a half mile away. It was cooking, the smoke pitch black.

Chris and I began burning, one eye on the flames and one on the ground ahead of us. We were carving a burned-out barrier to stop the flames before they reached town.

When you use a drip torch, whatever you drip it on will usually take a while to catch, like a birthday candle struggling to light. Not now. Drip, *poof*! Drip, *POOF*! The ground was hot, the air was hot, the fuel was tinder dry. The flames sprouted full-grown, with that velvety sound a stove burner makes when you light it. The whole damn desert floor was aching to go up.

Sweat popped on my forehead and rolled down past my Ray-Bans. The heat was pressing through my yellows, unusually strong. Your body is like a thermostat; it can sense when heat is about to inflict serious damage. There wasn't a lick of cool in the air.

The other bell ringing in my head concerned the brush to our right, the patch we'd just come through. It was double overhead, twice as high as me, and it was thick. I didn't like the look of it. As a hotshot, you have to know where your escape route is. But just charting a burn line through this stuff was tough going.

The flames were pouring down the hill to our left. Chris and I were lighting the oak brush, drifting south, trying to keep ahead of the line. But the inferno was shooting through the stuff horizontally, just eating the brush.

The fire was moving so damn fast. It was two hundred yards away now and the noise was building. A mountain-sized lion roaring, that's what it sounded like. Burning embers flew through the air, lighting up spot fires ahead of the fire wall.

I was dripping gas to my left when something happened. Suddenly the torch was spitting out flames and brush was lighting off in front of my face. The *air* was catching fire. I knew this happens when there's too much gas in the mix, but it was still unnerving.

Panic was shooting through my brain. In my shaking peripheral vision, I could see that the fire line was now fifty yards away.

I heard Chris yelling behind me.

"Ditch it!" he yelled. "*DITCH! IT!*" I froze for a half

second. *Is he really saying...?* I turned to see Chris put out the wick on his torch, then draw back his right arm as if in slow motion, the torch hanging off his fingers. Then his arm whipped forward and he heaved the thing toward the wall of flames. Its red metal spun against blue sky.

Only in the most dire circumstances do you ditch your drip torch. It's what keeps the flames off you. It's what kills the fire. Dropping it is like handing your gun to the Nazis. But I did't want the torch to explode and cover me and Chris with fuel.

The oak brush was angling in from our right. It was as if the landscape were closing in on us, wrapping us up, delivering us to the fire. Twenty yards away was a modern two-lane highway that takes you straight to Phoenix, where the world is modern and safe. But in this tiny little closed-off space Chris and I were alone. No helicopters, no tankers, no other crew. Just the fire and us.

The blaze was thirty yards away now, the flames two or three stories high. I snuffed the wick on my drip torch, reared back and launched the thing straight at the fire.

"*Gogogogo!*" Chris yelled. I turned and ran, Chris five yards behind me.

I began to hear a particular sound. The sound of a freight train. *Fuck no*, I thought.

An out-of-control wildfire that is bearing down on you makes a sound like a freight train, or really a hundred freight trains shooting out steam at high pressure. Not only that, but each burst of sound seems to spawn three more, until there's this infinitely expanding roar ripping in your ears.

That's what I was hearing now as I scrabbled toward the brush.

Hotshots believe that once you hear that sound, you're nearly out of time. If the wildfire caught Chris and me, we'd either be dead or suffer 100 percent body burns. There were no other options.

I had a crazy thought: What if I turned, sprinted toward the wall of flame, and jumped through it. If you're lucky, you come out the other side with 30 or 40 percent burns across your body. Better than 100 percent. Better than death.

But I couldn't do it. I had a fast image of bending down to pick up Michaela and her seeing my face and my hands being patchworks of keloid scars and her screaming. When you jump through, you have to give up your face. There's no way to protect it.

I kept running.

I hit the oak brush at full sprint and threw my left shoulder into it, nearly losing my balance and toppling over. The brush was just so strong. I began bulling my way through, grunting and breathing hard. The roar behind me made it hard to think. The thicket was like a living thing and I couldn't get through it.

"Push, Chris!" I shouted.

"What?" he yelled.

"Push, motherfucker!"

I felt Chris smash his forearm into my pack and begin shoving me forward. He grunted. As I barreled ahead, my sunglasses were ripped from my face. Oak brush swept across my eyes and I whipped my head down. The branches were cutting at my face, but I barely felt it.

With the two of us pushing with all our might, we were progressing inches at a time. The harder we pushed, the more the brush sprang back. It was a terrifying feeling, the one from the dream where something is coming for you but you just can't move.

The inferno was blasting in my ears. I didn't want to turn around. The heat pressed through my Nomex shirt and scorched my back.

We were caught by branches as thick as your index finger. This shit had been growing and coiling together for fifty years. It was hopeless. We'd gone in at the wrong spot.

Chris was shouting, "HELP! *HELP HELP HELP!*" behind me.

I pushed again and tripped. I was on my knees now. I stayed down and shoved ahead, my shoulders clearing a path. After a few minutes, I was completely exhausted and could hardly move. I felt caged inside the brush, with the fire approaching from behind. Chris came around to my left and shouldered his way past me, then turned and started dragging me out of the scrub oak. He was shouting, but now his voice was sucked in by the howling of the fire. Our brothers were somewhere through the wall of brush but no one could hear us.

I scrabbled across the ground as Chris hauled forward. I saw daylight ahead and the dark flat shape of asphalt.

"Five feet!" I screamed to Chris. I heard the brush behind us starting to cook off like a brick of firecrackers on the Fourth of July. *It's too close*, I thought. *It's going to catch us down here and we're going to go up like stacked wood.*

I was exhausted from the six-mile run earlier that day. My lungs were shredded. I forgot about Michaela and my mom and all that stuff. Something darker and more primitive took over.

I tried to move forward but I had nothing left. Chris

was pulling me toward the highway. With one last grunt, he jerked me free of the brush. The air was cool out here and I took a deep breath as we stumbled ahead. My hands touched dirt and we both collapsed to the ground, ten yards short of the highway. I could hear Chris rasping next to me.

The air was clean and not too hot. We sucked it in greedily. I felt pure animal joy surging through my gut.

Made it. Made it. Holy shit, we got out of that alive.

We were on all fours, crouched on the highway about thirty yards from where we'd gone in. Out here it was a normal Tuesday afternoon. Trucks zoomed around in the distance. I heard choppers in the air. Human voices not too far off.

I looked back at the brush we'd just escaped and as I watched, it changed from light brown to orange and there was a sound like a drawing-in of breath. And then the oak brush went up with this great throaty bellow.

The flames crowned and arched over the highway ten yards down from us, the heat scorching our faces. The sky above turned an intensely bright orange for two or three seconds and then snapped back to blue.

Chris and I picked ourselves up and walked down the asphalt, then turned to watch the fire eat into the trees on the other side. It was making this crashing sound, like a monster chewing through a forest.

I heard someone coming up on us. It was Jesse.

"What happened to you two?" he said, all casual.

Chris and I looked at each other and I saw his eyes crinkle under his helmet and suddenly we were giddy. We laughed like jackals. I pointed back. "What happened to us? You see *that*?! Dude, we were in there a minute ago."

Jesse grabbed me in a bear hug. He did the same with

Chris. Together, we watched the fire leap the highway and go running down the other side.

Before that day, I'd never thought of going home while on the job. I'd been tired and worn out and homesick and physically broken before. But I'd never said to myself, *Okay, that's all for me*. That thought had just never crossed my mind.

But now I wanted nothing more than to get in the buggy and drive and find Michaela. My body was shaking and I felt my knees wanting to buckle. When you get that close to burning up, your body thinks you actually did get burned up—there's a memory of something that never happened. Images, sensations. When you feel a wildfire that is thirty feet tall, half a mile wide, and maybe two thousand degrees hot, your body is so terrified that it keeps telling you one thing:

Run.

I seriously thought about it. Seriously. I'd always said this was my dream job and these were my brothers and I would have laid my life down for them without a second thought, and I meant every one of those things. But I found out on Granite Mountain that day that there's something deeper inside you: the desire to take another breath.

I was having trouble controlling the amount of fear that was in my bloodstream right then. I breathed out in choppy little gasps. I couldn't get enough air into my lungs.

Stop it, Brendan, I said to myself. *Right now. It's okay to be afraid, but you can't be scared. Breathe, motherfucker. Get another drip torch. Man up.*

After two or three minutes, Chris and I got up off the asphalt, had a drink of water, and went back to the fire line. Later, we found our drip torches. They were there all right, but in pieces, the metal twisted and crisped out. We laughed as we held them up and showed each other.

Someone handed us new torches and we hiked down to flank the fire, and we said not a word more to each other about what had just happened.

This was twelve days before Yarnell.

CHAPTER ONE

I grew up about four hundred miles from Prescott, in a town called Oceanside, California, in a nice middle-class neighborhood not too far from the beach. We—my mother; my older brother, Chad; and I—lived with my maternal grandma and her second husband, my step-grandfather, who I called Grandpa. I was a beach rat who loved the sand and skateboarding and all that. A typical blond, blue-eyed SoCal boy.

I remember myself as a happy kid, full of joy. I got good grades, even though I was the class clown. My nickname was "BB" because I zinged around like a tiny copper-plated bullet. I had more energy than a two-thousand-volt wire, and that sometimes got me in trouble.

It was innocent stuff, at least to begin with. In second grade, my friend and I would hide under the beanbags in the classroom and giggle as the teacher called out our names, growing louder and more worried the longer we failed to respond. "Bren-*daaaaaaan*!" She couldn't for the life of her imagine where the little blond boy had gotten to. We'd be under the bags in the cool darkness, stifling our laughs. When she found us, we'd shoot out of there and run for the hallways.

I needed the energy, because life with my mother was different. You needed a lot of stamina just to keep up.

My mom is an original California free spirit. If you gave her three or four hours to do anything she wanted, she'd find the nearest beach and wander it, picking up seashells and staring at the waves. Or she'd dive in and surf.

Mom always had her eyes on the horizon, waiting for the next big thing to come along: the next city, the next adventure. Restless. She was always looking to strike out on her own, but it never seemed to work out.

One time when I was six, my mom got invited to a birthday party in Vegas. She left on a Thursday and was supposed to be home on Monday. Monday came and went. No mom. Tuesday, Wednesday, same thing. It turned out she'd liked Vegas so much she'd decided to stay a few extra days, hanging out with old friends who introduced her to new friends.

Finally, after the better part of a week, we got word she was coming home. I went to the airport with Grandma and my brother to pick her up, super excited, and when she came down the runway, she was in a wheelchair. Turns out she'd gone Jet Skiing on some lake near Vegas, taken a bad fall, and broken her back.

My brother and I thought she was paralyzed or something. We bawled our eyes out at the sight of her.

That was Mom.

My mother wasn't happy in Oceanside. When I was eight, she found a place in a neighborhood called Libby Lake and said we were moving. I'd never heard of Libby Lake and I didn't want to leave Grandpa. He was as good as a father to me. I wanted to hold on to that kindhearted old man for as long as I could.

But my mom was determined. So we packed our few belongings and got ready for the move to the cheap duplex she'd found for us. I got over my fear of leaving Grandpa and, as moving day got closer, got more and more excited. What was the new place going to be like? Who was going to be my best friend?

After we squeezed into the duplex, one of the first things I learned about my new neighborhood was not to go near Libby Lake Park after dark.

"Why?" I asked Chad.

"Just don't," he said. Chad was tall and strong and usually pissed off, so I listened to him. Later I learned that the authorities would drain the lake every so often and find needles, guns, and once in a while a dead body. It turned out that Libby Lake was the kind of place you move away from, not to, but my mom never did things the way most people do.

It was a Latino and black neighborhood and I definitely stuck out. I had this Irish name, Brendan McDonough, that might as well have been Walter McWhitey. I was the first white kid a lot of the neighborhood dudes had any dealings with. I'd grown up playing flag football in Oceanside with black and Samoan kids, so it wasn't really a big deal for me. But Libby Lake was that times a hundred. I remember counting seventeen ice cream trucks one day, and hardly any of the drivers spoke English. I learned quickly to order my favorite ice cream bar *en español*.

Libby Lake was more chaotic than my old neighborhood. Things touched off quicker. One time, I was playing outside on the street with my new friends when a door banged open with a noise like a gunshot and a kid came running out.

Right behind him was his uncle with a belt hanging from his left hand, the heavy steel buckle dangling at the end. The boy had stolen something and the uncle was screaming in Spanish that he was going to beat him like a dog.

My mouth instantly went dry and my heart beat fast. I wasn't used to this kind of drama. My grandfather was a peaceful man who hated confrontation. I'd never even been spanked.

Now I looked at the faces of my friends as this kid was screaming bloody murder and running for his life. They were calm and smiling; their arms were balanced on the handlebars of their bikes and they were leaning forward to see what would happen next. Would Jose get away this time? Or would Uncle Rico give him a good whipping? It was like they were watching a football game. Who would win?

Oh, man, I thought to myself. *I guess this is normal in Libby Lake.*

Even the nice things turned weird, like neighborhood dogs. My friends told me about one called Fluffy, who we'd hear barking behind his chain-link fence. But Fluffy, despite his name, was a psychopath. Every time he got loose, kids would run down the street yelling, "Fluffy's out! *Fluffy's out!*" Everyone tore ass for a safe spot and prayed that Fluffy wouldn't find them. That dog would bite anything that moved, and you'd have to stay inside until the owners came home and rounded Fluffy up.

When one lady who lived nearby confiscated our soccer ball and cussed at us for being bad kids, we didn't take it lying down. We walked over to her house, found her family's car parked in front, and proceeded to go totally apeshit on that thing. Five other kids and I crawled on it like we were playing king of the mountain. *Bang*, we jumped on the hood. *Boom* went the roof as we launched off it like a trampoline.

Pure boy adrenaline. When the cop sirens sounded in the distance, we howled and ran off.

I guess I had some anger in me. I didn't know from what. But I was up for destruction.

It wasn't long before I went looking for a friend. A different kind of friend, you could say. Like, a calming influence.

I saw my chance one day walking home from school. There was a yard at the corner of my block that was the biggest in the neighborhood. "That guy's been here since the dawn of the dinosaurs," my friends said. The neighborhood must have gone downhill since then, because his property was strung from corner to corner with strands of barbed wire. (Again, not really a normal thing on the street I'd grown up on.) Between the planks of wood you could see what he was protecting. Fruit and nut trees: orange, lemon, almond. It was beautiful back there.

One day we were walking by the barbed-wire house and I heard a meow. I instantly went down on my hands and knees and at the bottom of the fence I saw a kitten's pale orange paw sticking out. Apparently the old man's cat had a litter, and one of them was calling to me. My friends were like, "What are you doing, Brendan?" but something about that kitten's crying touched me. I spent twenty minutes on my hands and knees trying to draw it out, long after my friends had left. The kitten was too scared, though, and wouldn't come to me.

I ran home and burst into the little two-bedroom we were staying in.

"Mom, Mom, I found a kitten behind the barbed-wire fence. If I can get it out, can I keep it?"

My mom looked at me dubiously.

"Please? I'll take such good care of it. *Pleeeaaase?*"

We had an old cat, but that was my mother's. I wanted a pet of my own.

"If you can get a baby kitten to leave its mom and come to a complete stranger's house? Sure, baby. You can have it."

I grabbed a handful of cat food and headed out. Two minutes later I was back at the fence. I smoothed out the dirt at the little depression under the fence and put three pieces of kibble there. I waited.

It was summertime. People passed me on the sidewalk. Some kids called to me to play basketball. But my eyes were focused on that kibble.

I called the kitten and made noises with my lips. I didn't care how I looked.

But nothing. The kibble sat there like three little rocks.

I looked through the fence and saw the lemon trees waving in the wind. I sat on my butt and called again.

Suddenly, a little orange paw darted out and tried to scratch the kibble back.

"That's right," I said. "Get some lunch."

I saw the kitten's nose sniff the food. I could see it was a little tabby cat, maybe eight weeks old.

I reached out and grabbed the kitten and pulled it under the fence. It struggled at first but I sat on the sidewalk and scooped it into my arms. It felt so soft. I put the little guy in the hollow of my neck and calmed him. Then I walked home, happy and proud.

Three days later we discovered the kitten had fleas. There were things biting us all over our bodies. We had to leave the duplex and move back to Grandpa's. Worse, I had to give up the kitten. It killed me to do it and I cried some hot tears, all right, but Grandpa was allergic to cats, so it was either him or the cat. Grandpa won.

That one hurt.

CHAPTER TWO

My dad wasn't in my life. He lived in Boston, part of a big, scrappy Irish clan that didn't have much in the world.

Dad was a street guy, a real hothead—but as he explained it, if you weren't a hothead in Southie, you might not live to drink your first beer. One time, when he was fourteen, he was walking on his block with his twelve-year-old brother when an older guy started hassling them. My father didn't miss a beat, just turned and walked straight up to the guy and punched him in the face. It was on.

Fifteen seconds later, the older guy was pummeling my father something serious. My father turned his head and called to his brother, "Hey, go home and get a knife out of the kitchen drawer, will ya?"

His brother didn't understand. "Whatcha want a knife for?"

My father whacked the guy in the ribs and then turned back to his brother.

"Because if I start losing," my dad said, "I want you to give it to me."

My uncle ran home and got the knife. By the time he got back, the fight was over and my dad had won. A not-atypical afternoon in the neighborhood.

So that was Dad, and that was Dad's neighborhood. I loved the stories, but I would have rather had him around. My mom left him when I was two. Don't know why they met and don't know why they parted.

But I knew this: He had problems with drugs. And his dad had passed away at a young age, and my father and his four siblings grew up without a man in the house. Those two things, and the hot temper, were part of my legacy, I guess.

They say the Irish are repressed, but sometimes you repress things for a reason.

My maternal grandparents had money. My mom didn't, and she also didn't have a good way of getting enough to support us. She and my grandmother always scrapped about this. Grandma probably could have given her $50,000 to put down on a house and get started in life, but that wasn't her way. She'd give you $10 here and $25 there, after much pleading. That infuriated my mother. She felt like she was being treated like a ten-year-old kid.

Their arguments were the background music of my childhood.

My mom also had bouts of depression. I can remember finding her in bed at noon, and her mumbling to me that she needed a rest. I knew somehow that mommies were always supposed to be up at that time, working or making lunch and not lying in darkened rooms with all the drapes pulled.

It got her down. At times, she couldn't get her head off that bed. It was as if her body was being weighed down by a special gravity that I couldn't feel. I could see it in her pretty face and her exhausted eyes.

After Libby Lake, there would be other efforts to strike out on her own. It seemed like my mom could handle living with her parents for only a year or so before trying to get away. We moved into a series of bad, crime-ridden neighborhoods, each one sketchier than the last.

When I was around twelve, we moved to a place three hours by bus from my school. I couldn't believe it. I didn't want to leave my friends and the teachers I loved, but there was no way I could do six hours on a bus every day. I ended up not going to school that first day. Just stayed home and watched TV. Afterward, my mom drove me back and forth to the new school, but I'd lost interest in the whole thing. I went from being an A and B student to getting C's and D's.

There were days when my mom wouldn't even argue when I told her I wasn't going to school. Instead, she'd say, "Hell with it. Let's go to the beach." Escape to the sand. But besides making me a primo skateboarder, it didn't do much for my education.

The next move, when I was eleven, was to a place called River Oaks. One of my friends from middle school lived there, and when Mom announced that we had to go somewhere, I said I'd follow her to River Oaks, but that was the only place. It was a pretty run-down neighborhood, but at least I knew someone there. She agreed.

Chad, though, wasn't having it. His attitude was *I'll stay right here with Grandpa and Grandma, thank you very much*. I guess he was being smart. It was one of the things that would drive a wedge between us.

I protested, too. "Why do we have to leave?" I demanded. "All my friends are here!"

"Because we gotta go. I can't stay here anymore."

It's not fair, I thought. And it wasn't.

But I knew and my mother knew that I was coming with her. I could never leave my mom. If she said, "Brendan, get your stuff, we're moving to the dark side of the moon," I would have bitched for a while, then grabbed my toothbrush and my favorite toy and waited on the front stoop. I would choose my mom over anything.

But Chad was done with us. I had to move to a whole new neighborhood and try to make a new set of friends and avoid getting beaten up, without my big brother to help me. Chad was drinking by then, getting into squabbles and becoming part of the SoCal punk scene. He had a lot of rage that he got out in his music. He disappeared one time and my mom told me he was in something called "anger management." I thought, *Yeah, Chad could use that.*

It hurt when Chad chose my grandparents over us. I think he saw how close my mom and I were. We had that bond that he and she never had, or that they'd lost. He was sad and bitter that I was her favorite.

I'm not sure if Chad ever said those words, but I could read it in his eyes.

I think it kept him from loving me, to be honest.

River Oaks stays in my memory because that's where I smoked weed for the first time. The kids I was hanging out with were passing a joint around one night when I should have been at home. When it came to me, I hesitated, then said, "Why the hell not?" I put the joint to my lips and took a hit. *Ahhhhhhhhh.* The anxiety and sadness that were more and more a part of my life began to recede far into the distance. I loved weed from the get-go.

We lasted a year in River Oaks before my mom had to swallow her pride and go back to Grandpa's. Each time, I returned a little more streetwise, a little angrier.

Six months later, I was twelve years old, lying upstairs in my bed reading a book about a boy who survived in the Canadian wilderness with just the hatchet his mother had given him. I loved that book; I imagined I was the little boy hacking off tree branches for firewood and shivering with cold.

Voices came up the hallway, Grandma and my mom fighting. I closed my eyes and tried to block out the sound by humming. It worked for a while. I leafed through the pages of *Hatchet*, humming a little louder when Grandma's screeching voice rose higher.

Then I heard my mom say two words that caused me to sit straight up on my bed.

"I'm leaving!"

I'm leaving? Not *we're* leaving?

"Brendan!" I heard her call, her voice full of anger and misery.

I tossed the book on the blanket and ran downstairs. My mom was standing there, shaking, her eyes angry, her mouth tense.

"Brendan, I'm going away for a while. You're staying here with Grandma."

I opened and closed my mouth a couple of times, but nothing came out. My mom walked by me to her room and began throwing some clothes in an old bag. I stood in the doorway.

"Mom, take me with you," I said.

Her back was to me. She zipped up the bag—*zzzzzap!* I flinched at the sound.

"Mom, pleeeeease don't go." I followed her out to the driveway. She didn't so much as glance at Grandma, who was yelling from the kitchen, "If she wants to go, Brendan, let her. We don't need her here."

My mom threw her bag in the backseat of her purple Dodge Intrepid, which had dull metal shining through where the paint had worn away. She came back to me and bent down and grabbed me, and held my body to hers. She must have said something to me, but there was a buzzing in my brain and I didn't make out the words. She stood up, jumped in the Intrepid, and threw it into reverse. Five seconds later, she was gone in a swirl of dust.

When we spoke on the phone afterward, she tried to explain: "I had to go alone, Brendan. I *have* to try something new. When I'm settled, I'll come get you."

I'd never really had my dad. I'd lost Chad. I'd lost my crazy friends from Libby Lake. And now, by far the worst of all, I'd lost my mom.

I sat on the driveway crying until my grandpa came out to get me. He was a gentle, good-hearted man. He patted my shoulder and told me to come inside. I went up to my room and cried.

She was away six months, in Oregon. I cried myself to sleep the first four or five nights and dreamed of the day I'd make enough money to buy a big house, big enough for my mom and dad and Chad and Grandpa and Grandma. Mom finally came back after being in a car accident where she broke her back again.

When you've been left behind as a child, that pain never leaves you. Even if you don't know that memory is there, it is. I would learn that soon enough.

CHAPTER THREE

My mom did come back. I was happy to see her, but I wasn't the same kid she'd left behind. I'd had that first toke of weed when I was twelve, and I'd liked it. I was getting into fistfights now and then. I hated to see anyone mistreated and I enjoyed smashing my fist into the face of people I didn't like: bullies, racists, dumbasses.

The following year, my mom's birth father, who lived in Prescott, was diagnosed with cancer. The doctors were giving him six months to live. She wanted to be near him at the end, so she announced one day that we'd be moving to Arizona. She went on ahead the spring of my eighth-grade year. I graduated middle school, then packed up and followed her, a week after the Fourth of July.

I didn't want to go. In fact, I was dead set against it. To a SoCal kid, Arizona is like something out of the Middle Ages. I'd been to Prescott once with my grandma a year before and I'd thought to myself, *I wouldn't make it even one year in this town*. Now I was going to live there.

"Are you kidding?" I yelled. "There's nothing in Prescott

except rattlesnakes and hillbillies. What am I supposed to do there?"

My mom reminded me that it was her last chance to be with her dad.

"Besides," she said, "it's a chance for a fresh start."

I laughed bitterly. Fresh start, my ass.

Grandpa and Grandma drove me to Arizona. When we stopped for food in one of the mountain passes, I could feel that the air was thinner. My heart raced a bit.

The closer we got to Arizona, the more depressed I became. As far as I was concerned, there was a whole lot of nothing east of LA. Roads winding through snowcapped mountains. Town names like Bullhead City and Fort Mohave. We passed through places that looked like they closed after dinner. No kids. No sidewalks. No damn beach.

When we rolled into Prescott, I thought, *Oh, hell no*. The "downtown" (later I would learn it's called "Whiskey Row") looked like something out of an early John Wayne movie. The whole town seemed to be a bunch of dirt roads and cowboys. People were seriously walking around wearing ten-gallon hats, like it was 1876.

I felt out of place before I even got out of the car. *I will never live in a little hick town like this*, I said to myself. *I need sand and water*. I'd inherited my beach-bum genes from my mother and I loved heading to the ocean and just letting the waves ease my mind. The desert heat and the high altitude wiped me out.

. I spent the first couple of days sleeping, depressed about moving to this back-of-beyond place and starting over again. After a while, I began exploring the town, or what there was of it, and tried to get my bearings. It was shocking how different Prescott looked to me: I was used to hanging out with blacks, Mexicans, Samoans, and anybody else who'd fallen into California's melting pot. Here it was mostly Caucasians. But not my kind of Caucasians. *These people*, I thought, *are straight-up* white.

Prescott teens hunted in the hills around town with crossbows and rifles. They knew how to quarter and skin their prey before taking it home. If they bought a pickup truck (and what else would they buy?), they knew how to take apart its engine and fix it. They rode broncos and bulls at the town's annual Frontier Days, the world's oldest rodeo, then drank at the bars along Whiskey Row. The local heroes weren't skateboarders or rappers. They were the cowboys, the roughnecks, the undersize 170-pound linebacker from Prescott High who got a Division I scholarship because he was the toughest goddamn player in the state.

I spent the summer hanging out at the skate shop across from our apartment block. I was looking for friends, but it didn't happen. Californians have a bad reputation in the small mountain towns of Arizona; either they're rich, arrogant snobs who pay $3 million for a mansion in the hills, or they're poor SoCal rejects who smoke weed and don't pay their debts. It was tough to live down that reputation.

In August, I went to Prescott High as a freshman. Most of the kids there'd had their friends since third grade. They'd all come up together. I was the outsider with the laid-back accent who wore pulled-up black socks, Vans, Dickies shorts, and flannel shirts. You could say I was a bro dude—half my style borrowed from the black guys and gangbangers of SoCal, half from the surfers in Oceanside.

It didn't go over so well. The other kids were dressed in Wranglers, cowboy boots, cowboy shirts. My clothes were wrong. My hair was wrong. My voice was way wrong.

So I fell back on what I knew: partying. When I was thirteen, I had my first drink. Sailor Jerry rum and Coke. It was back in Oceanside over winter break. I was hanging out with my brother and his wild friends and they offered me a cup, and then another. After my second, I puked my guts out all over the pavement. My mom had no idea.

I was already a little wild. My philosophy was: Anything worth doing is worth overdoing. I wanted it to be known that Brendan McDonough never backed down from a fight, never saw a party he couldn't take over, and never said never.

The first friends I found at Prescott High were exiled Californians like me. We formed our own clique. I started staying out late, partying in the hills around town. The hills were a good party spot because it was easy to see any cops coming up the roads. They rarely bothered us there anyway. We'd look up at the stars, pass around a joint, and talk shit.

Through freshman and sophomore year, my drinking and drugging behavior got crazier, my friends got sketchier, and my grades dropped like a rock. My mom was truly unimpressed with me. Not only was I repeating her worst mistakes, I was topping them. I'd stumble in at two a.m. on a school night, ripped out of my mind.

"Brendan!" She'd come storming into my room. "What the fuck is wrong with you?" My mom could really tear into me. I argued for as long as I could before I passed out, and then she was talking to a corpse.

But I had another side to me that I like to think I inherited from Grandpa. I still carried within me an old-fashioned sense of duty. If he was in line at a grocery store and there was a single woman who couldn't pay for her groceries, he'd slip the cashier fifty dollars to cover her—he was that type of guy. He looked out for other people; to him, that was just part of being a man. I'd absorbed that growing up.

In middle school, I'd volunteered to go to LA and work in one of the big homeless shelters there. I went along Skid Row with some other volunteers handing out sandwiches, offering people a place to sleep and shower, and doing anything we could to get these men and women back on their feet. Skid Row isn't some romantic hobo camp, believe me. It's hard-core. A lot of addiction, bipolar disorder, random violence. I wasn't a churchgoing Christian, but I knew about Jesus and I really wanted to live out his message. At the shelter, I bathed and cleaned the feet of homeless men and found them new shoes from truckloads of shirts, socks, and sweaters donated by DC, a skate clothing company. Some of the men cursed at me as I did this; others thanked me humbly.

I was grateful for the chance to help. It doesn't matter how bad your life gets, there's always someone else who's got it worse.

In Prescott, I went to little out-of-the-way trailer parks, one of them occupied by World War II veterans who'd fallen on hard times, and cleaned up their yards and landscaped them, putting in trees that would blossom and give the people there something to be cheerful about. I volunteered for the Special Olympics. And at Prescott High, I made a point of standing up for anyone getting bullied. Nothing pissed me off like a bunch of idiots or gangbangers tormenting a kid who was weaker than them.

I never gave in. I took a lot of pride in that.

Still, I was lost. I didn't know if I wanted to be a drug dealer or a priest. Both had their attractions.

The truth was, despite my good intentions, the party monster side of me always dominated. And it only got worse. My mom was working at a plant nursery and took side jobs doing landscaping. She'd managed to rent a house for us by working her ass off, but she was too damn tired to control a six-foot teenager with a mind of his own.

So the party monster won out.

There was one last thing, besides the cowboy boots and the pickup trucks and World's Oldest Rodeo, that was different about Prescott. You lived with fire. It was always on the edge of your life. Sometimes you'd be walking to school and you'd smell smoke. This was different. It tasted like burned pine needles and scrub oak. The wild.

Prescott did regular controlled burns in the hills around town to get rid of the dry and dead brush that could endanger the city if it was hit by lightning or touched off by ricocheting bullets (everyone in Prescott went target-shooting in the hills). The smoke would come down the slopes and settle in the streets. You'd be in school learning geometry and you'd start choking on these invisible fumes. Or there'd be a real wildfire and you'd hear the sirens blaring all over town, and the local news would be full of people talking about how close the flames were.

I was a beach kid from Oceanside and I had no idea what was going on. To me, "nature" meant fresh marijuana.

Still, fire was always with me then. It was like a signal from over the hills that the sun sank behind every night. Despite the buildings and the Thai restaurants and the shopping malls, it said, *You are living in the wild. One day, sooner or later, you'll come face-to-face with the natural world. And the natural world does not play by human rules.*

CHAPTER FOUR

By the time I was fourteen, my mom was at her wits' end. She began looking around for a way to get me off the druggy trail I was following and found something called Fire Explorers. It's a program designed for teenagers who think they might want to be firefighters. It could have been for budding taxidermists, for all my mom cared. So long as it kept me on the straight and narrow, she was happy.

The last thing I wanted to do was spend my evenings in another classroom with a bunch of fire geeks. But I went along, hoping to get her off my back.

On the first day of class, the instructor handed out a textbook, *Essentials of Fire Fighting.* It was 716 pages long. I nearly fainted. I've never been much of a reader, and I thought, *What the hell am I going to do with this thing?*

The instructor finished handing out the books. "This is not just another textbook, like you get in school," he said. "This is the book being used in the fire academy right now. It's life and death."

I opened the monster and turned to the first page:

This manual is dedicated to the members of that unselfish organization of men and women who hold devotion to duty above personal risk, who count on sincerity of service above personal comfort and convenience, who strive unceasingly to find better ways of protecting the lives, homes and property of their fellow citizens from the ravages of fire and other disasters... THE FIREFIGHTERS OF ALL NATIONS.

I read the paragraph again. Something there appealed to me. The idea of a worldwide brotherhood, maybe. Of service. Of sacrifice.

I had never sacrificed anything in my life. I had nothing *to* sacrifice. We were too broke for that. But here was a profession where I could save others and still live out an adventure.

Fire Explorers was the first thing in my life I took seriously. I loved the long, punishing workouts and the push-up contests. I liked the discipline. I even liked the technical stuff. I learned how to tie different knots—a bowline, a clove hitch, a figure-eight follow-through, a becket bend. I became a deft hand with an ax. I could search a room engulfed in flames just by touch (though we never trained with live fire).

Even if I was hungover or high or depressed, I never missed a class. I decided I wanted to be part of this brotherhood. I wanted to be a firefighter.

But what I *was* was a drug dealer. It was the only way I knew to make decent money. By seventeen I was running a thriving business in pot and pills. If you were looking to score in Prescott in 2010, I may have supplied you with weed or Molly tabs. Primo stuff, too. I was really good at my job.

I had to make money somehow. And being a drug dealer is a great way to make friends. I had clients who were star football players, physics nerds, rich Cali kids. They invited me to their parties. They paid pretty much whatever I asked them to. For a stoner like me, it was a dream job.

But my addictions were getting worse. I sampled my own product so much that it seemed I was stoned from morning until I passed out in bed at night. School was an afterthought and my grades bottomed out.

My mom would ground me, or attempt to. But she was too worn out from working to chase me down and actually make the punishment stick. My senior year we ended up living a few houses down from Prescott High. I took advantage of this by running home during lunch break, taking some huge rips on my bong, snorting a few pills, and then heading back for my last classes. A midafternoon pick-me-up. My go-to pills were OxyContin and Percocet, which I got dirt cheap.

One day I took one too many hits on the bong and crawled back to school late for the bell. The next period was computer science, a class I was barely passing, and I needed to be in there. I skulked outside the window trying to catch the eye of one of my friends. Finally, one of them spotted me. I gestured for him to open a window in the back of the room. He got up, strolled over to where I was, and slid the window up. I was going to go in commando style, hit the floor on all fours, and crawl to my desk. With the Percocet in my blood, this made perfect sense to me.

I managed to pull myself up to the sill and slide my body through without alerting the teacher, but on my way down to the floor I knocked a chair over.

BAAAAAMMM!

The teacher whipped around. I was lying on the floor, laughing my ass off.

I imagined that I was building my legend. But really I was trying to escape my life. My mom's unhappiness. Her screaming at me as soon as I walked in the door about my pissing my life away, being a degenerate, and so on. The fact that my father would have walked by me on the street without recognizing me. The fact that my brother would have done the same just because he didn't care to be associated with me.

I graduated high school in 2009. With school, my life had some structure. But after graduation, I joined the small Prescott community of tweakers, dealers, and future inmates that centered on Whiskey Row.

A typical weekend night from 2010:

I was invited to a party at a mansion in the hills, one of the million-dollar homes I would one day keep from going up in flames. My friend picked me up in his lifted Toyota Tundra and I jumped in there with four other guys. When we got to the party, the driveway and nearby streets were packed with Lexuses and Porsches. I walked into the mansion and all I could think was *Whaaaaaaat*. There was a dance floor bigger than any apartment I'd ever lived in. A live four-piece band that could really play. Men with strange masks on their faces and women in dresses made out of shiny patches stitched together with black lace. Guys wearing high-end watches that cost more than pickup trucks.

One of my friends went to the bathroom and came back with his eyes wide.

"Dude, there are hidden cameras in the bedrooms."

"What?! Why?"

"Why? Because this is a swingers party, man!"

We looked around. All the men seemed to be around fifty and all the women around twenty-one. So obviously at some point in the night, there was going to be a joining of these two populations.

We had to think this over—why had *we* been invited?— and smoke some weed on the patio. It was about eleven o'clock and the deck was thick with people popping pills and swilling champagne.

Out of nowhere, I felt something smash into my right cheek. I staggered back and saw a stranger in a white shirt getting ready to hit me again. His eyes were bloodshot and there was a tie pulled halfway down his shirt.

My buddies bent the dude over the railing. People were screaming as his feet tilted up in the air.

"Throw him over the railing!" one of my buddies yelled.

The patio looked out over a cliff of scrub, landscaped rocks, and cacti.

"Toss him!"

"Hell no," shouted another friend. "It's thirty feet over there!"

We dropped the guy back on the patio and turned to see the place in riot mode. Inside there was chaos. Chairs arcing over the dance floor, cocktail glasses being smashed on people's faces, figures wrestling in the half darkness. The band was running for their lives.

Had the kids figured out what was going on and revolted? I never found out. Didn't matter who started the fight, because we knew whose side we were on. My friends and I waded into the brawl, throwing haymakers at the older dudes and knocking one or two out. Then, with bodies scattered across the polished floor, we ran for the exit.

It was all good times until it wasn't. By the time I was eighteen, it seemed no night was complete unless I'd blacked out or knocked someone's front teeth in. Several ended with me being chased by the cops. I even had a fake name—Chad, easy to remember—that my friends called me on certain nights so that, should things go south, the authorities wouldn't be able to track me down.

But I still wanted to be a firefighter, and directly out of high school I went to the fire academy in Prescott. There was a guy there named Tony Sciacca, who was enrolled in a class on structure firefighting. Tony was a local hotshot legend. He'd started out at the bottom, working forest fires, and he'd built himself up so that he was now leading a Type 2 incident management team, which means you're certified to handle most kinds of natural disaster, even up to FEMA-level catastrophes.

I told my mom that Tony was teaching at the academy. Mom, who's nothing if not direct, went to talk to him behind my back. The next day Tony found me in class.

"I hear you want to be a firefighter," he said.

"Yes, sir."

"Okay, but do you want to sit on the couch and watch Lifetime movies, or do you want to actually work?"

I had no idea what he was talking about.

"Why don't you become a hotshot?" he said.

"A *what*?" I had never heard the term before. Shows how clueless I was.

"We fight forest fires," Tony said. "Sometimes we're out in the woods for two weeks at a time. You're choppered in with some chow and your gear and you live in the wilderness and you actually work."

It sounded like heaven. I'm not saying Tony white-washed things, but he definitely emphasized the good parts of being a hotshot: the camaraderie, the outdoor life, the nonstop action. He also made it sound *easy*. I was so green, I thought, *Wow, you get paid to go out into the forest and kill big-ass fires? Sign me up*.

I would soon learn how wrong I was.

I didn't want a desk job. I didn't want to be a supervisor or a captain or chief. I just wanted to start out as one of the youngest firefighters in Arizona history and put in twenty-five years of hard work, fighting every kind of blaze there was. I wanted to be the kind of veteran with two knee replacements that some young buck calls "Gramps" one morning and asks what time he's due back at the retirement village—before I leave him gasping on a brutal mountain run. A grizzled old bastard who tells stories around campfires about the wickedest fires he fought. Who's earned the respect of everyone.

That was the sum of my desires. To be a firefighter's firefighter.

In the spring of 2010, I was on my way. I was enrolled in an EMT course, which every structure firefighter has to pass. My mom had been hired at a fire service station out near Chino, working the front desk at their main offices. I'd taken a wildland firefighting course at the Prescott Fire Center and aced it. I felt like I was ready to start fighting fires.

But in my EMT class, my lifelong difficulty with book learning finally caught up with me. I'd made it through high school without ever learning to study. I was quick and had a good mind, but I just couldn't sit with a book in my lap and read. I'd never been diagnosed with ADD, but I was always convinced I had it—maybe that was the origin of my boyhood nickname, BB. As hard as I tried, it seemed my eyes jumped away from the page before I got the sense of what was on it. But I don't want to blame some disorder. I didn't push myself hard enough to overcome that.

Whatever the reason, halfway through the EMT course, I flunked out. This derailed all my plans to join the Prescott Fire Department. I saw my buddies finishing the class and getting jobs with fire departments and crews. Believe me, it was depressing as hell.

Then I remembered what Tony Sciacca had told me. And I realized that hotshots aren't required to pass an EMT course. I was so relieved. Here was a way into the brotherhood. The last way for me.

My mom kept an eye on openings at a Type 2 crew station in Chino and let me know when they were looking for guys. She put in a good word with her bosses at the Arizona State Forestry, which ran that particular crew. *I'm a shoo-in*, I thought. I knew I'd be good at the job, too. I felt like all I needed was one clean break and I'd be done with drugs forever.

When the time came, two of my friends and I applied for the open slots at a different Type 2 Initial Attack crew, basically highly trained firefighters who are among the first responders to a fire. I checked my application twice before sending it in. "In three months," one of my friends told me, "we'll be out on the line killing fires together."

The competition was intense. Every other kid in Prescott grows up wanting to be a firefighter, or at least the kids I knew—the ones with no college degree and parents who were barely making it themselves. The cowboy jobs are gone. The army and marines take you away from your family for months at a time. Everything else is minimum-wage jobs.

But being a hotshot? That was the dream. And the slots filled up quick.

A month later, the list for the new hires was out and I went to the Forestry station to confirm that my name was there. I was feeling good. *This is the first day of the rest of my life*, I thought. Like my mother, I'm addicted to that feeling of a fresh start.

But before I even got a look at the names, a supervisor pulled me into his office. "Brendan," he said, "I don't know what happened, but you're not on the list. We'd really like to hire you, but if your name didn't show up, my hands are tied."

I was dumbfounded. How was I not on the list?

"Can you call the forest service and find out what's going on?" I asked.

The supervisor shook his head. "Even if it was a clerical thing, they won't let us take you. They'll tell us to go back to an old list and hire from there. It's procedure."

We found my application and went over it line by line. There it was, on page two. I'd mistakenly clicked "one semester" of training instead of "one year." One little pull-down question and I was done. It was my own damn fault.

I was completely gutted. But I didn't want to whine about it.

"I appreciate your time, sir," I said to the supervisor. "If anything changes, please know that I'm ready to go. And thank you."

He nodded. I walked out to my car. It was a blazing Arizona day, the sky so big you feel you're floating faceup in blueness. But for me everything had turned dark. I got in my car and cried my heart out.

CHAPTER FIVE

I decided that God wanted me to be a party person. What else could the botched application mean? My dreams were dashed and so I dived back into the drug scene. I went back to popping Percocet and Oxy to balance out the depression I was feeling.

The week before high school ended, I'd met a girl named Natalie. She was blond with blue eyes, funny as hell, a little ditzy. I charmed her with texts and phone calls and soon we were a couple.

I wasn't the best boyfriend, that's for sure. Natalie didn't know about the OxyContin or other pills, but she watched me smoke joint after joint, turning into a stoner. I soon broke up with her.

Not too long after that, Natalie informed me she was pregnant.

The baby was mine. Of course it was.

I knew Natalie wasn't the girl I was going to marry. But there I was. After she told me, I drove over to her house and her mom and dad were waiting for me at the kitchen table. We sat there not looking at each other, as if someone had died. Her dad glanced at me and I could tell I wasn't exactly his idea of a son-in-law.

Brother, I thought, *I am right with you on that. I am not ready for this.*

"I want to have the baby," Natalie said.

Her parents' eyes went a bit wider.

"Well, are you two even together?" her dad asked. "I thought you'd broken up."

I looked at Natalie. I could tell that behind her brave face, she was scared. I felt like it was time to man up.

"Sir, as of this minute, we're back together again. And I'm going to do everything I can to give that baby the life I never had."

Her dad nodded without much conviction and I gave Natalie a hug and was out of there.

I wanted to be a man of my word. I took any job that I could find—mostly odd jobs in construction and landscaping. I kept telling myself that when I put enough money together, I'd go back to school and start on a real career. But I'd heard my mother say the same thing a hundred times, though until we moved to Prescott she had begun living out what she said. I knew school wasn't my salvation. I wasn't cut out for book learning.

I so wanted to do the right thing, but I had no guidebook on how to go about it. I started going to the gym that winter, trying to get in shape. I stopped seeing the worst of my stoner friends and cut down on my drug intake. I was doing the best I could in my new role as an expecting father.

I knew I had no right to be a father in my present condition. But no matter what I did, I saw my daughter's life becoming a remake of mine: absent dad, struggling mom, minimum wages, a restless wandering that led nowhere. I couldn't handle that. I didn't want another generation of McDonoughs to be too strung out for the good life.

Natalie was a few months from delivering and I became desperate to get work, any work. I walked into McDonald's and filled out an application, but nothing happened. The same story with In-N-Out Burger, Costco, and Walmart. It was a shock to me. I was nineteen years old and basically unemployable.

Depression shadowed my days. Some mornings I'd lie in bed and feel like I couldn't get up if the sheets were on fire. I saw no way a good thing could happen in my life for the next forty years. It was all going to be black, depressing, drug-addicted shit, and nonsense.

And then I got arrested.

CHAPTER SIX

It was the typical thing: You do insane shit every day and then you get busted for something completely ordinary. Four months earlier, my buddy and I had been leaving a Walmart, stoned out of our minds, when he'd spotted a convertible sitting in the lot with its top down.

"Hey, Brendan, look at this," he called out to me.

I looked over. There was a GPS unit, a nice one, sitting on the guy's dash. And a radar detector.

"Should I grab it, dude?"

I was floating on Planet Stoner. "What?"

"The shit inside. Should I grab it?"

"If you have the balls," I said. "Which you don't."

I was just busting on him. We didn't steal things. We were partiers, not thieves.

I got in my car without a second thought. Out of the corner of my eye, I saw my friend plop into the passenger seat with the GPS unit and the radar detector in his hand.

Whatever, I thought. We rolled out of there to another party and I forgot all about it. Later on, I stuck the GPS under my bed and never used it. It was a goof, a stupid dare.

I don't approve of stealing things, but really, grabbing a GPS was pretty low on the totem pole of what we were doing at the time.

Cut to four months later.

A friend from high school returned from college and we decided to meet up at the gym owned by our old wrestling coach. We'd goof around and lift weights. I drove to the place and slapped hands with my friend and his dad, who was a mentor of mine from high school, and then we went into the gym and started lifting. That's when three guys in Dockers, long-sleeved shirts, and ties walked in and said, "Is Brendan McDonough here?"

I walked over, still breathing hard from the workout.

"I'm Brendan," I said.

They showed their badges. Prescott PD. "You're under arrest," one of them told me.

I was so ashamed. My face burned. My friend, his father, and my old coach looked at me and you could tell they were embarrassed to be there, to be seeing me at such a low moment in my life.

The funny thing is, I thought they were busting me for selling pot. Turned out it was the GPS sitting under my bed that had done me in. I was charged with a felony: receiving stolen property. The cops had gotten my license plate number from a surveillance video and had been following me around for months, thinking I was the head of some major theft ring. How they managed to miss my rampant dealing and out-of-control drug use is beyond me.

I spent the next few nights in jail over Christmas. I saw another guy who'd been arrested at the same time I was get released in the morning, but my mom wanted to teach me a lesson. She refused to bail me out. I spent my time teaching other inmates about how to get federal aid for college. Later I'd run into one of the guys I met that night and find out he was enrolled in school because of my advice. I got a kick out of that.

But mostly, I felt that my life was essentially over. *Deadbeat dad. Felon. Loser.* Those were the words that floated through my mind as I sat on my concrete bunk.

The DA tried to get me and my buddy convicted of a string of robberies that we had nothing to do with. He was asking for fifteen years for both of us. But there was no evidence—because we hadn't done the crimes—and the judge threw out the charges. I was left with one felony count of trafficking in stolen property. I pleaded guilty, my first conviction. Because I'd shown some direction in my life—illustrated by the fire academy and the junior ROTC I'd completed in high school—I was given probation. If I stayed clean, the charge would be knocked down to a misdemeanor within a few years.

But, still, I was a felon. I hated that word. I hated being known as a thief. It was another black mark on a life that was going nowhere.

CHAPTER SEVEN

When my daughter, Michaela, was born on March 2, 2011, I was there. I picked her up for the first time and a strange feeling came over me. I couldn't look her in the eye. I felt so weird in her presence. It was like I'd already let her down just by being who I was. I couldn't take the innocence in her eyes, the not knowing. I knew what she was in for, and it wasn't pretty.

Her eyes were so pure. It was heartbreaking to me.

I thought about suicide often, especially after another rejection on the job front. It was better to erase myself before my daughter got to know what a no-account loser I was. Maybe then, she could make up stories about me: He was misunderstood; he tried but never got the breaks. She'd have these little legends to comfort her.

Meanwhile, my mom was done with me. She'd kicked me out of the little house we were living in and I went to stay on a buddy's couch. I had one bag of clothes, a couple of pairs of sneakers, my toothbrush and razor, and that was about it. I really didn't have a single dollar to my name.

I kept telling myself I was done with drinking and drugs.

I'd be at a party flying on Molly and telling myself, "Okay, this is it. Tomorrow I'm going clean."

That would last twenty-four hours. When you start to go sober, you realize that there's nothing in your life to replace the drugs. You get clean and then you wait for the good feelings to come flooding in. But they don't. The old bad feelings come instead: You're a failure. You're a deadbeat dad. You suck.

And you're like, *Ohhhhhhhh, right.* This *is why I do drugs.* And you go out and find a buddy and pop some pills. Three weeks go by and you're hooked even deeper and you see no way out except death.

My depression got so bad, I even smoked heroin for the first time. A sweet numbness crept over my body and all my worries seemed to float off like birthday balloons.

I can't lie. I loved heroin.

That spring, after my daughter was born, I found myself in Phoenix in a trailer park. I was there picking up some heroin from a dealer who I'd scored from before. The trailer was a mess: food cartons everywhere, broken Xbox games, dirty clothes thrown on the floor. The sun was baking through the roof. It smelled bad.

I was sitting on the couch with my buddy. We'd scored the heroin but were too high to move. We were watching the dealer, a Mexican gangbanger, play with his gun. He was dressed in a wifebeater and jeans with a chain dangling on the side, and he was spinning the nine-millimeter around his finger, pointing it at things in the apartment—the TV, the window, whatever. He was silent, his expression alternating between bored and pissed off.

His two kids, aged maybe four and six, were playing an Xbox to my left, yelling in Spanish, and working the controls like maniacs. The dealer's girlfriend was dozing on the bed.

There was a knock at the aluminum door. The dealer stood up and stuck his gun in the back of his waistband. He walked to the door. He seemed nervous.

"Uh, are we about to get shot here?" I said to my buddy. He shrugged.

I heard a voice outside. Ragged, quiet. "Got any?"

It was a crackhead, apparently. The dealer walked out and he and the crackhead started arguing.

"Fuck you, little bitch!" the drug dealer shouted. "You come here, you pay my price."

The crackhead said something unintelligible. The dealer yelled something in Spanish.

Mexican standoff, I thought to myself, but it wasn't funny. I looked at the girl on the bed and the two kids. I wondered if the dealer had pulled his gun out. The walls of the trailer would offer zero protection against any bullets flying our way.

What am I doing here?, I asked myself. *This is a scene from someone else's life. Not mine.*

"Let's go," I said to my buddy.

We went out, shuffled around the dealer and the addict— he was a white dude with squared-off glasses wearing a tank top. The guy was begging now. We got in my buddy's car. I'd sold mine a couple of weeks before and used the last of the money to buy the two packets of heroin in my pocket. Later I managed to scrape enough together to buy an old Ford Explorer, but right then I was depending on friends for transport.

If this ain't bottom, I thought, *I don't want to know what is.* I had nothing to call my own except Michaela. I was so, so tired of the life I was leading. Who would care if I gave it up? No one. Least of all me.

Three days later I heard about an opening for hotshots.

CHAPTER EIGHT

The jobs weren't with Prescott Hotshots, the oldest crew in town. They were with Granite Mountain Hotshots. The new guys. The upstarts.

Granite Mountain was already a minor legend in hotshot circles. The crew evolved from a Fuels Management crew in 2001, to earning their official Hotshot certification and status in 2008. It was the first hotshot outfit attached to a city fire department. Most crews are primarily state or county outfits. Granite Mountain was special. It was the only city-employed hotshot crew and the first outfit to have that distinction.

Granite Mountain was known for going anywhere and fighting any kind of fire. High desert, low desert valleys, grasslands, salt cedar riverbank, big timber, ranchland, wildland-urban interface, didn't matter; if you called Granite Mountain, they came. Arizona, California, Montana, or Minnesota, they got the call. They got helicoptered out to jobs in the remote wilderness and stayed there for two weeks, living like Lewis and Clark out on the frontier.

The supervisor of Granite Mountain was a guy named

Eric Marsh. I'd heard of him. He was a North Carolinian, an outdoorsman, movie-star handsome, former rugby player, a degree in biology from Appalachian State. He'd helped create the Granite Mountain crew nine years earlier. It was his baby.

I wanted to be part of it. Honestly, I wanted anything that paid $12.83 an hour and more with overtime. If it involved risking my life, I really didn't give a damn. Bring it on.

There was another thing about hotshottin' that appealed to me. I'd grown to love the Southwest: the desert, the toughness and humility of the people, the self-reliance. I wanted to feel I was a part of that. Maybe I needed to fit in, but I was tired of being known as a California stoner, and of everything that went with that: the flip-bill baseball hats, the "What's up, brah?" accent, all of it.

I wanted to grow up, I guess. Become a man and all. And I wanted to be accepted where I lived. I was too broke to afford a horse, so I couldn't be a cowboy. And there is nothing more Southwestern than being a hotshot.

The day I decided to try to get a job at Granite Mountain, I was working at a ranch, digging holes for a fence surrounding a chicken coop. I'd just been let go from a job at a car dealership where I was in charge of giving oil changes; they couldn't keep me because my terrible driving record meant I couldn't get insured. If I didn't get the Granite Mountain job, I had three realistic options: drug dealing, day labor, or suicide.

I drove to the station in my beat-up Ford Explorer. Granite Mountain operated out of a big shedlike structure made of galvanized metal painted blue, surrounded by a chain-link fence. I drove by the gate and my heart was beating like I was driving in the Daytona 500. I slowed down, did a U-turn, then rolled back, looking at the place out of the corner of my eye.

I could see a few guys walking in and out, getting stuff from their trucks. They wore black T-shirts and green cargo pants and they looked like Navy SEALs to me. Super fit. Tanned. Clean-cut dudes.

I was thin, strung out, and sleeping on my friend's couch. I'd smoked heroin the week before. My drug spiral was out of control. So I was scared to go in there. I was scared of not being good enough. I was scared they'd look at me and say, "Brendan McDonough? You have *got* to be kidding me."

In my six years in Arizona, I'd learned about many things. I knew my way around a bong, the best places to score X wholesale, and the pitfalls of the Arizona court system. But I knew nothing about the wilderness. The only time I'd ventured out into the hills and desert surrounding town was to get wasted. I hadn't been on so much as a single hike into the Prescott National Forest. I had no idea what the wildland *was*.

These guys did. They risked their lives out there.

You don't belong here, I said to myself.

After my third drive-by, I got mad at myself. *Goddamn it, Brendan, get in there for your daughter.* I jerked the wheel and rolled through the gate.

I got out of the car, almost shaking. I was wearing an old tank top and jeans, and out of some kind of Dale Carnegie impulse I decided to tuck the tank top into my jeans. Then I walked into the station.

For some reason, Abraham Lincoln came into my mind as I entered. Just his nickname, Honest Abe. My life was a series of lies and contradictions, and I was sick of it. *Just be like Honest Abe*, I told myself. *Just tell the truth no matter what. Put it all out on the table*.

I walked through the doors and found myself in a little

hallway. The first thing I saw was a guy I'd taken my EMT class with, and I smiled in relief. "Hey, Daniel," I said. "Do you still have any positions open?"

He gave me a strange look. Later he told me that I'd tucked my tank top into my underwear by mistake, and they were visible above the waist of my jeans. What a champ.

"Hey, Brendan. Ah, no, sorry, we don't. We're all filled up."

The floor seemed to sink away. I felt defeat just wash over me.

"Okay, thanks," I said. It had taken all of five seconds. I turned around.

To my right was an open doorway. As I approached it, a man walked out.

"Hold up," he said. "You're looking for a job?"

I didn't know it then, but this was Eric Marsh. He was tanned and fit, like everyone in the place, but a little older. His eyes were kind. His voice had a bit of a Southern twang at the end of the sentences.

"Yes, sir," I said.

"We've got one spot left open. You have your certifications?"

I couldn't believe what I was hearing.

"Yes, *sir.*"

"Okay. Can you do an interview now?"

Now? I felt the fear come back full force. But I made myself nod.

"Yes, sir. Whatever works best."

He nodded back, his eyes appraising me. "Come on in."

I walked in after him and saw that there were four other guys in this little office. It was a bare-bones place with an old brown couch to the left and a gunmetal-gray desk to the right. I sat down on the couch and two hotshots sat on the other side of me. Eric pulled up a chair and sat about five feet from me, with two other crew members leaning on his desk on the other side.

I was surrounded by these intense-looking dudes. It was intimidating. Despite my years of fire training and EMT and the rest, I felt like an imposter. I vaguely recognized the guy to Eric's right, too. Were they aware of my past? Did they know I'd been a drug dealer?

I was insanely nervous. My hands seemed like two enormous blocks of wood; I didn't know what to do with them. My throat was parched and felt like it was closing up.

Eric asked me my name and when I said it, I felt a kind of hush or chill in the room. The guy on his right stared hard at me, like he'd heard of me, and not in a good way.

I ignored him and answered Eric's basic questions: social security number and all that. We went through my credentials and Eric seemed impressed. I explained that the reason I'd flunked out of the EMT class was that I wasn't much of a book person. Eric nodded. I'd enrolled in another EMT class and was passing so far.

But I felt the questions Eric was asking weren't the real test. He was studying how I reacted to him.

Abe Lincoln, I thought. *Tell the truth*.

"Is your driver's license good to go?"

My heart sank. No, it wasn't. It was suspended. I fessed up.

I felt someone laugh and the guy on Eric's left rolled his eyes.

"I paid the tickets, but I didn't know I had to go to class after that. I'm getting it worked out, believe me."

Eric looked down at his clipboard.

"Have you ever done drugs?"

My gut tightened right up.

"Uh, yeah, I have."

"Which ones."

Abe Lincoln.

"Weed, Ecstasy," I said.

The guy next to me shook his head sadly.

Eric's face was unreadable. "Anything else?"

"Some pills here and there. But I've been clean for a few months."

I couldn't bear to tell him about the heroin. There's honesty and there's job suicide. I had to be on this crew.

"Do you have any felonies, Brendan?"

Damn it.

"Uh, yes, sir, I do."

Someone to my right—I didn't want to look—snorted in disbelief.

I explained what had happened with my buddy and the GPS. I rambled on about how I was on probation and if I didn't violate the terms, it would be knocked down to a misdemeanor. But I could hear my voice. Spouting technicalities.

Eric's eyes held mine.

"Brendan," he said, his voice calm. "Let me ask you a question. What is integrity?"

I was caught off guard.

"Integrity?"

"Yeah."

I was stumped. This I'd never expected. Some words jumbled out of my mouth, "honesty" and "character" maybe; I was just blabbing anything I could think of. But I had the feeling everyone in that room knew that I had no idea what the word really meant. Not in the way these men did. Integrity had something to do with the way these guys lived, why they trusted each other, why they were willing to put their lives in the hands of their brothers.

And I had no clue.

I could feel the skepticism in the room.

Eric turned and picked up his office phone and called human resources for the city and talked to a woman there about my felony conviction. I could tell how the conversation was going. The woman on the other end was telling him to drop me and get another body. A traffic ticket was no big deal, but a felony? That was a killer.

I felt a headache starting way down at the back of my neck.

He handed the phone to me to explain what was happening with my driver's license. I told her I was working on getting it reinstated and asked her please not to kill my chance at a job over simple stuff like this. The office was silent, waiting. I handed the phone back to Eric and he said "Uh-huh" a couple of times.

Finally, he hung up and looked at me. "It's not a deal breaker."

I breathed out. I felt I had to speak up. I owed him that. *If I get in, I cannot let this man down.*

"Listen, guys," I said. "I've made a bunch of mistakes in my life. I've done some stupid things that I'm ashamed of. But I have a two-month-old daughter, her name is Michaela, and I'm trying to give her the things I never had. I'm not going to let her down. And because of that, I won't let you down."

Eric nodded. I would later learn that he'd had some bumps in his own road. He'd battled a drinking problem for years before beating it. He knew about second chances. Eric's wife let me know that he saw a lot of himself in me.

"Okay," Eric said. "We'll give you a shot."

I leaned my head back and closed my eyes. The relief was physical, better than any drug I'd ever taken. I thanked the guys and shook everyone's hands and made some more promises. Then I got the hell out of there before they could change their minds.

Almost any other day, if I'd walked into Granite Mountain, I wouldn't have gotten a job. Five members of the crew had left for opportunities elsewhere or because the work was simply too grueling. Granite Mountain needed bodies. At nineteen, I would be the youngest man on the crew.

I felt so happy. I had no desire—and no money—to go and have a beer or a toke to celebrate. The first thing I did was call my mom, who I hadn't spoken to in weeks, and tell her the news.

"I'm so happy, Brendan," she said quietly. I could hear the caution in her voice. I had always been a guy with big plans, and she'd become wary of my pronouncements, but I could tell she wanted to believe. So did I.

There was one problem. I didn't have any money to rent a place, and I knew the training was going to be exhausting. I had to be rested and stable in order to keep the job. Sleeping on my buddy's couch and eating junk food wasn't going to cut it.

There really was only one other option.

"Mom, can I come back home?" I said.

Silence.

"You bet," she finally said.

I hung up and cried. I felt like I'd been standing on a cliff, slowly leaning over until I was about to fall into oblivion. And at the last minute, a hand had reached out and snatched my hand, pulling me back. I didn't know if it was luck or God or just chance, but I was so filled with gratitude that it was overwhelming.

That night, I went to Natalie's place and picked up Michaela. I held her in my arms. For the first time, I felt worthy of that trusting look in her eyes. I just stood there, holding my daughter, crying tears of joy.

It was the first time I really felt like a father.

CHAPTER NINE

Mentally, I was ready for Granite Mountain. Physically, I wasn't even close. I was a pale, thin, 145-pound party hound. I'd never run more than two miles in my life. I'd been a stoner for eight years and a drinker for six. I was detoxing off heroin. And I could barely run a half mile without getting a stitch in my side.

I thought fighting fires would be the hardest thing about joining Granite Mountain. I was wrong. There would be days in the coming months when my buddies and I would close our eyes and pray for a fire, just so we wouldn't have to go through the gut-wrenching training that Eric had designed for us.

I was the last rookie to be hired that season. There were four other guys who'd been training for a week already and had started bonding with the veterans. My first week, I had the feeling I was trying to sneak one more Oreo into the package, and that Oreo didn't want to fit. I was the man on the outside.

Besides that, I'd known a couple of the guys casually for years, and they had my number. They knew the old Brendan from parties and brawls and high school gossip, and they weren't buying the new one. A couple of them told me straight up that they were going to try their damnedest to get me to quit.

They thought I was a punk. No one expected me to last a week.

The first day I did part of my pack test with a full-time veteran named Clayton Whitted, a strong Christian man who'd already passed the test but had volunteered to do it again so I'd have someone there to motivate me. The pack test measures muscle strength, endurance, and aerobic capacity. Basically, it's a test to see if you can handle the job physically, and the requirement is to finish a three-mile hike with a forty-five-pound pack in forty-five minutes.

We did the test on flat ground. I was wheezing from the get-go. I finished the hike with about two minutes to spare. Not good. Clayton was waiting for me.

"That was a bitch," I said.

"That," Clayton replied, "is about the easiest thing you'll do as a hotshot."

I didn't believe him. I should have.

Day two, I showed up at the station early and by nine a.m. we were off on a training run. PT was next—physical training to build us up for the days when we'd be fighting a fire for fourteen or sixteen hours in the middle of nowhere with no one coming to relieve us. It was hot as hell, creeping up toward a hundred degrees. We got in the buggies and drove to the Brownlow Trail, near Pioneer Park in Prescott. I got out of the buggy and thought, *Oh no.* There wasn't a shade-giving tree anywhere in sight. You could see heat waves shimmering two feet off the ground. *We're gonna roast*, I thought. I put some chewing tobacco in my cheek and tried not to think about it.

We started running, making a tramping noise on the packed dirt. The trail was fairly flat, which I was thankful for, but it was still brutal, full of switchbacks and bordered by pollen-bearing bushes. One of the things I'd hidden from the group was that I was asthmatic. For years, I'd used an inhaler. One look at that brush and I could feel my lungs twitch.

I've never been much of a runner. And now I was trying to keep up with a bunch of guys who were in hella good shape. It felt like I'd caught a refrigerator on my back.

Two miles out—with five more to go—I felt someone behind me. I looked back. It was this veteran, Chris Mac-Kenzie. He was a black-haired guy with tattoos and a big mustache. And right now, he had a pissed-off look on his face.

"Dude, pick it up!" he yelled.

Guys were passing me on the right. Just blowing by me like I was using a walker. And they were the new guys, too, rookies like me. I swore at each one under my breath, *Motherfucker, I will get you back for this*.

I was ready to topple over from the heat and sickness. My blood was beating in my temples. I turned back around and ran faster.

We ran mile after mile, the dust floating up and choking me. I was gasping for breath and I could see the gap forming between me and the guy ahead of me. Bad news.

Come on, Brendan. Stop bitching and MOVE. But my body was drained. Just lifting my legs was agony. Getting them to move faster was not going to happen.

Just then I heard someone running up behind me.

It wasn't a jogger; it was Eric. The man had steel springs for legs; he could run all night if he needed to.

I felt a wave of anxiety. *Is he going to let me go right now? Did I blow this already?*

To tell the truth, some part of me was half hoping that was the case. My lungs were shredded and my legs were screaming. If he let me go, there'd be less shame in leaving.

Eric fell in beside me. He didn't say a word. We ran through the Arizona backcountry in silence, my nervousness growing, the two sides of me debating whether it was better to be fired or to keep going. As we approached the last mile of the run, I had to slow down even further. My legs felt like they were going to lock up on me. I was embarrassed, the breath coming out of my mouth in ragged bursts. Eric was barely breathing hard.

Get it over with and fire me now, I thought. Or maybe I should just quit and save some face.

I was about to tell Eric I couldn't run anymore, that I was done. Just then, he leaned over. "If you give up on this run," he said quietly, "you're gonna quit on your daughter every day of your life."

I finished the run.

After we stopped, I put my hands on my knees and wheezed. My lungs felt like they were full of steel confetti. I didn't even know lungs could hurt, but they did.

Eric was standing, barely breathing hard. He took a swig from a water bottle.

"All right, guys, push-ups."

"He said what?" I whispered to the guy next to me.

The guy ignored me and dropped to the ground. I felt a bright pain in my forehead, but I got down on my knees and got into the push-up position. Eric was counting out. My arms were shaking.

It was a full hour of calisthenics.

The other rookies were in better shape. They'd gotten through their first week and were already starting to get conditioned. I'd basically come off the party circuit straight into marine boot camp.

I made it through the calisthenics and then the run back to the trucks. At times, I was half walking. Chris continued to harass me, snarling about how I was fucking up the crew. *Man, that guy* hates *me*, I thought.

We got in the buggies and drove back to the station, covered in sweat. We got out and I collapsed against the side of the building, sitting with my back to the corrugated metal, chugging water. The ground was cooking hot. I felt like I weighed six ounces and a good breeze would pick me up and carry me away.

Someone sat down next to me. It was Chris MacKenzie. He leaned back and looked up at the sky. I tried not to watch him. We were silent for a couple of minutes.

Finally, he spoke up. "Why don't you just quit?" he said.

I didn't understand why he was dogging me. But I wasn't giving in.

"Not fucking happening," I said.

Chris acted like he hadn't heard me.

"You're slow," he said. "In fact, I've never seen anything as slow as you. You look like a gazelle but you ran an eleven-minute mile today. Eleven fucking minutes."

I hadn't realized I was being timed. Damn.

"No offense, dude, but you run like you weigh three hundred pounds," Chris said. "You're wheezing. You can't carry your weight. You're going to be a liability to every guy here when we really get out fighting wildfires. Is that what you want?"

I closed my eyes and tried to block out the sound of his

voice. I thought of Michaela. I tried not to think of smashing Chris right in the face, which is what I really wanted to do.

I felt that if I opened my mouth we were going to fight. And I couldn't lose this job.

Chris leaned in toward me. "So let me ask you that question again. Why don't you just fucking quit already? You're never gonna be a hotshot."

I took another sip of water and waited for him to leave. Finally, with a snort of disgust, he did. I watched him go, feeling more alone than I had in months.

What if he's right, though? What if I get out there and can't hack it and someone dies because of me? How's that gonna feel?

That was just the morning. In the afternoon, we went out and fought a simulated fire.

The exercise had two objectives: teach the rookies like me what they were doing out there, and work on fuel breaks. A fuel break is a strip of land that's been cleared of fire fuel. If a fire comes roaring across terrain, a fuel break is supposed to stop it, or at least slow it down.

Eric set out different-colored flagging to represent a small fire: the green flag might be the eastern flank, the red flag the western flank, and so on. He was teaching us how to see a fire, how to get its size and its shape into our heads so we could fight it. So, in a way, we could outthink it. If we knew the shape of the fire, the fuel it was consuming, the terrain it was on, and the weather that was driving it, we should have an idea of how to kill it.

But that was way above my pay grade for now. That first

day, I was brute labor. Some guys took out their chainsaws and started cutting brush, while their partners hauled it off to a safe distance (this is called "swamping"). I was part of a dig team, using my Pulaski tool to root out the last of the vegetation from the firebreak. The Pulaski was a double-headed tool that had both an ax and an adze, which is a kind of narrow shovel. The thing had been invented by a forest ranger named Edward Pulaski a hundred years earlier. It just showed you how being a hotshot hadn't changed that much in a century—which wasn't the most encouraging thought. It was still a few men against a fire, with only a couple of modern tools.

I thought I'd worked my ass off doing day labor. I'd dug ditches, installed fence posts, and all that before, and I'd held my own. But the pace Eric maintained was unbelievable. The guys were digging like the fire was twenty yards away and getting closer. There was an urgency that I'd never been part of before.

"Let's go! Pick it up!" Jesse called.

The heat, the brutal work, the yelling. *Is this really the job?*, I thought. And this was just a trial run. This wasn't even real.

I'd imagined something different. I knew more about structure firefighting, where you're mostly hauling hose. But this was like building a house or something. Clearing the land. Digging the roots out. It was work.

I thought of Tony Sciacca and his telling me about being a hotshot. *That son of a bitch*, I said to myself. He was like the recruiter who tells the dumb young kid about how the marines get all the girls, about R&R in exotic places and buying a big lifted truck with your first check—and forgets to mention the drill sergeant and getting your ass shot at.

The guys worked without a break. The job was non-stop, you just kept hustling until your shift was over. I thought, *I'm sorry, boys, but I'm going to have to sit down.* I didn't, but I wanted to.

Chris saw me taking a little breather.

"Out drinking last night, rook?" he yelled, not in a friendly way.

I shook my head. I wished I had that excuse, but I didn't.

I couldn't picture the fire. There were going to be days when the temperature was hotter because of a blaze bearing down on us, and I didn't know how I was going to get through it. It was near a hundred degrees already. What would it be like when flames were a hop, skip, and jump away?

My feet were numb and my mouth was parched, but I worked my ass off. By four p.m., I was nuked.

Thank Christ it was a Friday. If the next day had been a workday, I doubt I would have made it out the door. I went home that night and just collapsed into my bed, not even bothering to shower.

CHAPTER TEN

I had all weekend to rest up. I spent most of it in bed. I didn't even want to think about a full week of training. My body was sore and brittle. I staggered to the bathroom and then back to bed.

As painful as it was, I never even thought of quitting. The guys who washed out of Granite Mountain had a tradition. They didn't walk into the station and resign to Eric. That would have been too humiliating, like failing manhood. Instead, rookies drove down Sixth Street late at night, hauled their gear out of their trucks, and threw it over the station's back fence. They were too ashamed to face the hotshots.

No way was that going to be me. On Monday morning, I pulled my shirt on, feeling like I was dislocating my shoulder, then thrust my legs into my pants like a senior citizen.

I looked at myself in the mirror. *Are you sure you want this?*

Yes, I wanted this.

I drove to the station, walked in, and said "Hey" to the guys in the locker room. No one said anything. Just nods. At best.

After a quick briefing, we got in the buggies and went right out on the trail.

When we lined up, I saw Chris fall in behind me.

This is bullshit, I thought. *I'm going to lose it and crack this man right in the mouth.*

I was even slower than I'd been on the first day. Every tendon in my legs felt like it had been sanded down, leaving the nerve endings exposed. The stiffness lasted for a mile, then I felt heat rippling up through my thighs. Then waves of pain.

Sweat was pouring down my face. Someone was charging up behind me. I stumbled and nearly fell to the ground. I heard Chris's voice.

"What the fuck, rook?"

I could feel my Irish temper burning. Short fuse. On any given Friday night, I would have turned around and it would have been on. But I had to control myself.

I straightened up and staggered ahead. Mile after mile. I could feel Chris getting more and more furious behind me.

Later, I would learn more about him. He was from Southern California and had been a hotshot there. He had the pedigree: engine work, helicopter work, seen every kind of wildfire. Cali has the oldest and the baddest crews in the country, because they have the big fires and the big populations and they have a tradition. So they've always set the standard for the nation.

Cali guys don't tolerate bullshit. And maybe Chris, seeing a fellow expat on the trail, was doubly disgusted: Not only was I a disgrace to hotshottin', I was a disgrace to SoCal hotshottin'. I was making his ass look bad.

Cali crews have a make-or-break attitude. They grind rookies until they snap or until they find a reason to like them. And one thing was for sure: Chris MacKenzie was finding no reason to like me.

"Get off this trail, rook."

"Fucking deadweight."

"*Move*, bitch!"

No one on Granite Mountain wanted me there. They weren't going to risk their necks to help me. Why should they? Case in point: my inhaler. I'd gotten one because I'd known we'd be out in the wilderness and I didn't want to have an asthma attack out there. At the station, it was easy enough to hide. Keep it in a pocket or in my locker and take a quick shot when no one was looking. But out on the trails, that's hard to do. There were a couple of times I had to use it. I literally could not breathe.

That afternoon, a hotshot named Jesse Steed walked over to me.

"Hey, Brendan. Do you use an inhaler?"

I felt caught out and a little embarrassed. How did he know? Someone must have told on me.

"Yeah, I do."

"You got asthma?"

I nodded. "Listen, are you gonna tell Eric?"

"I don't care that you have asthma," Jesse interrupted. "I care that you hid it from us. We're here to support you, Brendan. Seriously, what the fuck were you thinking?"

I shrugged. "That someone would find out and I'd lose my job?"

"If you've got a problem, especially a problem that affects the crew, we need to know. We'll help you all we can, but you've got to trust us."

I took the inhaler out.

"I'll throw this away, then."

I meant it. I'd rather take the risk of having an attack out in the woods than lose the job.

Jesse shook his head. "That's not what I'm trying to tell you. Keep it. Stay healthy. But don't keep things we need to know secret."

I nodded and stuffed the inhaler back in my pocket. I looked around, wondering who'd blown me in.

But it was my fault, really. I didn't have enough trust in anyone to admit I had a weakness. Addicts keep secrets. They lie. That was the code I knew.

That night the pain in my body was so intense I couldn't sleep. I tossed and turned. I'd gone to bed at ten p.m. but at midnight I was still staring at the ceiling. I had to be up at seven and if I didn't get any sleep, there was no way I was completing training.

Most people who detox from drugs do nothing for a week. I was doing it by working my ass off. My body was crying out for some relief.

You can do this, I said to myself. *You're worthy of being on this crew. Do not give up.*

The desire to be part of this brotherhood, to have a chance at the new life right in front of me, was overcoming my craving for drugs. I'd beaten my drug addiction, and it would never come back.

We ran endlessly, all over Prescott. People who were out hiking had no idea who we were. Some of them thought we were a soccer team training for a tournament. Some locals would be like, "Hey, thanks for what you're doing out here." But nobody really thinks about hotshots until they see a wildfire on the evening news, and even then we're hidden in the high timber, just doing our job.

Those first two weeks, one of the full-time veterans was paired up with me to make sure I didn't run off a cliff or collapse. These guys—I didn't know all their names yet—knew how to get inside your mind. But, unlike Chris, they were actually trying to help me, getting me to fight for the job.

"You done, McDonough? You had enough?"

"No, sir."

"You look like you wanna give up, rook. Go home and grab a beer. No one's gonna hold it against you, dude. You wanna go home?"

"No, sir!"

I asked myself, *Why are these guys trying to break me?* They were searching for my weak spots, and when they found one—my druggie past, my fucked-up family life— they pressed it until it was numb. *These guys want to know my deepest, darkest fears. Why, to use them against me?*

By Thursday I was feeling awful. My body was worn out. I was questioning whether I'd be physically able to even get through the training, never mind a wildfire.

We headed to Brownlow Trail for a run. I quickly dropped back to the end of the line. I was wheezing along, trailing far behind the other guys, even the other rookies.

Chris didn't bother to hassle me anymore. It was like he'd given up on me. Why waste time on a rookie who isn't going to make it? Weirdly, I almost missed his abuse. At least before, I had the feeling the other guys saw me as a threat to make the crew. Now they'd written me off.

CHAPTER ELEVEN

As the weeks went by, I felt myself getting stronger. My body was leaner and my thighs were thicker. Veins sprouted on my arms like underground rivers coming to the surface. A week later, I had to go out and get some new jeans because my old ones were too tight around my legs.

I also loosened up around the guys. When Chris or some other veteran started hassling me, my reaction was to take everything they threw at me and laugh in their faces. When we were getting ready to load into the buggies, I would yell, "Woohoo, gonna get some!" I'd do some whack hip-hop dances, throwing in a little robot, a little Cabbage Patch, in the locker room where we changed into our uniforms. I was unstoppable. I was the class clown again. I was not going to let them break me.

They sure as hell tried. When we climbed those hills, the boys gave me forty-pound jugs of water to carry, in addition to a fifty-pound pack. They laughed at how slow I was. They shook their heads in mock disgust as they passed me on the trail, sucking wind. "Mc Do Not" became my nickname, goofing on my last name.

"Mc Do Not climb hills!" they called out, cackling their asses off.

"Mc Do Not make this crew!"

"Mc Do Not have a future in hotshottin'!"

Eventually, "Mc Do Not" became "Mc Don't Wanna." But a nickname has to fit the person, and they grudgingly had to admit that I didn't quit on anything, so "Do Not" and the other variations had to go. Finally, they settled on "Donut," not only because I like donuts, but maybe because they secretly believed there was an obese man trapped inside my lean body.

That became my identity. When the hotshots introduced me to their moms or their kids, it was, "This is Donut." I didn't mind that, but later on, after I'd broken up with Natalie and was single, the guys' fiancées would introduce me to their hot girlfriends by saying, "And here's Donut!"

I had to pull my friends aside and say, "Dude, can you get your girl to stop doing that? She's killing me."

But I was Donut. Later, I'd get one tattooed on my leg. A new life requires a new name.

The first two weeks, I was too exhausted to pick up much about Granite Mountain. I was focused on surviving. But as I hung out more with the guys, and grew to like them more, I noticed things. First about them as a group. Despite all the jokes and ragging and constant one-upmanship, the Granite Mountain boys really cared about one another. I could see that. They were like family. If one guy had a problem with his girlfriend or the IRS or the courts, word would go around until someone was found who had some expertise on the matter. Then you'd see the two guys huddled at the long table in the break room talking it over.

These guys got together on weekends when they were off duty. They went to each other's cookouts. Birthday parties for the kids. Drinks after a hard job.

Not only did they care about each other, they talked about it openly. Later in my career, Eric gave a speech about integrity and friendship. "That's what this is all about," Eric said. "This job teaches you that the most meaningful thing in your life isn't money or a fast car or getting laid; it's earning the respect of your brothers. I mean it. There's nothing like man love."

I thought I'd heard wrong. A statement like that would get you knocked out in one of Prescott's cowboy bars. But Eric was a Southern gentleman and he rarely kidded.

I knew the statement had nothing to do with sexuality. It was a simple acknowledgment that the hotshots depended on each other for their lives and they would sacrifice everything for the next man.

I wanted that.

All through training, I'd been looking forward to my first fire, and three weeks in, I got one. Most of the crew was out fighting fires all across Arizona, but I needed to finish up one last class before I was allowed to go. I passed the class, and when the crew returned from the previous fire, within days I was off to Yuma with the crew.

I was assed out from the training and nervous about leaving Michaela. I spent so long saying good-bye to her that by the time I jumped in my Ford Explorer and headed for the station, I was late. When I got there, my fire captain—an older guy named Aaron Lawson—was standing in the parking lot waiting for me.

"What the fuck, McDonough?"

"Sorry, sir."

"We're waiting on your ass. Let's go."

My heart skipped two beats. My first fire! I felt the adrenaline surge in my veins.

"Time to battle Mother Nature!" I shouted to the other rookies. "Bring it on." They just shook their heads.

Inside the buggy, the guys were talking about Yuma. It was a salt cedar blaze. Salt cedar is an invasive plant that was brought to the States from the Middle East and Asia in the nineteenth century and grew like crazy, especially along the river and stream banks of the Southwest. It's not usually something that fuels up a major fire, but if it hasn't been burned in a while, it can be dangerous, tossing spot fires as far as five hundred feet. A spot fire is sparked by embers carried from the main blaze. If you get spot fires touching off behind and on both sides of you, it's easy to get trapped.

We headed out to Yuma, which is about a four-hour ride. Saw smoke on the horizon as we approached. It didn't look like much. Honestly, I was hoping for a monster, a big Type 1 fire where I'd have lots of responsibilities and I could earn some respect. But here the salt cedar was hemmed in by the local streams.

We parked the buggies about a mile from the fire line and humped in. I started in with the dig team, busting my ass with the Pulaski. When the sawyers needed me, I switched over to them. One guy, the sawyer, cuts the brush with his chainsaw. His assistant, the swamp brusher, pulls it a short distance away. The swamp brusher's assistant—me—does whatever the swamp brusher tells him to do: in this case, grab the piles of brush and pull them out of reach of the blaze. It's dry, dirty, thirsty, exhausting work, and it can wear you out quick.

The flames were eating through the salt cedar and you could feel the heat on your face. It was real now. You imagined that heat turning up fifty, a hundred, a thousand degrees. What would that do to the flesh on your face? What does a second-degree burn over 40 percent of your body really feel like?

I wasn't afraid but I was aware. The kind of fire I'd been reading about and imagining since I was fourteen was a hundred yards away. All the rookies were watching the fire line. We didn't know what to watch for, really. We had no idea what invisible forces would bring the flames to us. The veterans seemed to sense it in their bodies. They were relaxed. We were as keyed up as baby rabbits in a wolf den.

I spent the next two days digging fire lines and sweating my ass off. This was the grunt work of hotshottin'. We corralled the fire within a ten-thousand-acre sector and had it tamped down a day later. We loaded up the buggies and headed back.

I felt amazing. I'd earned my keep. I was on my way to being a hotshot.

Not all the rookies felt the same way. A few fires later, I was assigned to be a swamp brusher's assistant again. As I worked, I was watching another rookie; I'll call him Jack. Jack was a quiet dude who kept to himself, a college grad who had a business degree and probably should have been behind a desk somewhere writing nice things on a computer. He was a two-week wonder. He'd kicked my ass during training, running like a deer up those hills and hardly breaking a sweat. But ever since we'd gotten out into the field that day, actually working with tools in our hands, he'd been complaining that his feet hurt. *He'll get over it*, I thought. *When your whole body is aching, you can't worry about just one part. We'll all be there soon.*

The sun dug into our necks as we tramped across the low

desert, swamping. As the hours went on, Jack wouldn't stop about his feet. Hour after hour, it was "Man, these boots are killing me." *No shit, son*, I thought. The handmade boots we wore were extra thick and heavy, to withstand the heat we were walking through. Inside my boots, my feet were pale and sore and blistered, but it wasn't something you complained about. All the rookies were wrecked. Why bitch about it?

Carl, one of the veteran guys, was working as a sawyer, cutting the brush. I'd grab it, drag it away some, then pass it to Jack to throw over the cliff we were working near. The wind was gusting hard when I noticed Jack walking toward the edge of the cliff. When we'd hiked in, I'd seen that there was a sharp drop-off there, ten or twelve feet straight down. I called to Jack.

"Don't get too close to that cliff, dude."

"What?" he yelled. The wind was really moving and making it hard to hear.

I pointed at the cliff, then motioned toward me.

"That's a steep drop, bro. Just throw the shit up in the air and the wind'll take it over."

Jack looked at me with a blank expression on his face. I had the strangest feeling. *Something's not right with this guy*, I thought. But I had brush to haul and I went back to it. I glanced back at Jack between strokes and the second time I looked, damned if I didn't see the guy toppling back over the ridge.

I ran toward Carl.

"Carl, Carl!"

BAIRRR. BAIRRR. The chainsaw was roaring. Carl was in a trance.

I slapped him on the shoulder.

"What?!"

"Jack's down!"

"Well, tell him to git up."

"No," I yelled, pointing with my gloved hand, "I mean he fell over the damn cliff!"

"Oh, shit." Carl put down his 'saw and got on the radio while I ran over to the ridge. I reached the edge and looked over. Jack was laid out on his back, his right foot crossed over his left. He looked dead.

I ran down there and found him breathing fast. His pupils were dilated and he had a look of panic on his face. I didn't know if he'd broken his back or just knocked the air out of himself. I kept telling him to breathe, that everything was going to be all right. But in the back of my mind, I was watching him, wondering how exactly he'd tumbled over the edge.

"Did you feel that gust of wind?" Jack said to me.

I hesitated. "Yeah, man, I felt it."

"Knocked me right over."

There had been wind. But I had a gut feeling Jack had thrown himself over the cliff to get out of being a hotshot.

Some of the guys who'd been EMTs came running over and started checking him out. Another guy brought a spine board and we loaded Jack up and carried him out of there. Then we went back to work.

I kept my thoughts to myself. If a guy wanted out that bad and wanted to save face by risking his own neck, that was his business. Honestly, it was better if someone like that wasn't out on the line with us when it really counted.

But I'm like, *I'm a recovering drug addict and you're a track star, and you're bailing? Where's your heart at?*

We never saw Jack again. He gave his gear to one of his buddies on the crew and that was that.

Being a hotshot ain't for everyone.

CHAPTER TWELVE

'd broken my cherry. Back in Prescott, if someone asked me if I'd been on a fire yet, I told them yes. I felt good about it, but it wasn't like I went around bragging. I was working with hotshot legends on Granite Mountain. One fire meant nothing.

Five days after Yuma, we were in the station when Eric walked in.

"We're going to Chiricahua," he announced.

I knew there was a wildfire burning out of control in southeast Arizona, in the Chiricahua Mountains. Now we were being called in.

"Woohoo!" I shouted. I grabbed my bag and headed for the buggies.

We drove to the foot of the mountain range and checked in with Incident Command. It was evening, so we got our gear ready for the morning, then sacked out.

The Chiricahua Mountains are made up of a bunch of sky islands, tall rocky peaks surrounded by completely different terrain, like high desert or wild grasslands. It's a bunch of radically diverse habitats squeezed together. Perfect for Granite Mountain.

As we turned in, the guys were talking about the job. This was a real fire, a big one. Yuma had consumed 10,000 acres in a few days. Chiricahua was doing that every hour. It would soon grow to almost 250,000 acres, almost 400 square miles, thirty times bigger than Manhattan. And it was showing no signs of slowing down. There were hotshot crews from all over the Southwest already battling it. The elevations were crazy: The fire was burning from 1,000 feet to 10,000, up the steep, pine-studded mountain slopes. This job wasn't like going just outside Prescott and chopping down some trees. This was mountain-climbing country and hot desert and fast-fuel grasslands all packed into one mission.

The next morning, we were supposed to transport to the fire line. "We'll be taking a chopper in," Eric announced.

"Whaaaat?" I said. I'd never been in a chopper. Because I hate the damn things.

I had good reason. A lot of wildland firefighters have died in copter crashes. For years, the toll for aerial accidents was higher than that for fire-related deaths. In 2008, nine firefighters being flown in to battle the Buckhorn Fire died when their Sikorsky S-61 went down in the Shasta-Trinity National Forest. A lot of hotshots fear helicopters.

We loaded up on the aircraft, a little four-seater. The guy next to me, Travis Turbyfill, had been in the Marine Corps, and he nodded at me as I dropped into my seat.

The blood had completely drained from my face. I guess I looked pretty anxious, because he slapped me on the knee and gripped it.

"Don't worry, dude," he yelled over the rotor. "I was in one of these in the marines."

"Awesome!" I said halfheartedly.

"No big deal. If we go down, just keep your head tucked between your knees."

I gritted my way through the chopper ride, my gut like a yo-yo. When we landed, the crew gathered up, trekked out to the fire line, and set up camp, organized our gear, got a campfire going, and sat around it, telling stories. The sky above was so big it felt like you were floating in it.

The hike to the fire the next morning was a bitch of a trek. The sawyers had chainsaws on their shoulders, and the rest of us had extra water rations, extra chains, fuel and oil for the saws, plus our work tools. Each man was carrying at least forty-five pounds. We didn't have UTVs (small four-person off-road vehicles) or four-wheelers to bring stuff in. What we needed, we had to carry ourselves.

As we got closer, my body started feeling weird. Like woozy. I didn't know what was going on. *Is this fear?*, I thought. *Am I scared to get close to a big fire?*

Ever since I was fourteen, I'd thought of fire as violent and malevolent. I thought of it as a living thing, almost, something that was out to hurt me and the people I was trying to protect. I didn't think of it as evil, but to me it was kind of a predator.

But Chiricahua was my first time really seeing fire as something almost beautiful. To see it in this majestic place, away from humans, leaping from tree to tree, was to see fire as it had been before man ever existed. It was here at the beginning of the world. It was ancient, and it was so alive.

I guess it's the difference between seeing a Bengal tiger in a zoo, staring at you with hatred from between steel bars, and seeing it out in the wild, chasing an antelope. It's an awesome thing.

My hatred was slowly being replaced by respect. Chiricahua let me see fire as it had been forever.

That first day we dug line, with the fire a whole ridgeline away. But the following afternoon we got closer; we could hear the fire ahead of us. Feeding. A loud crunching, crackling sound, hundred-foot trees going up as the flames ate through them. Everything was bigger here: the timber, the distances, the fire.

Even the sounds. The flames out here in the forest sounded crisper, louder. I could see them crowning the trees a hundred feet up in the air, tongues of orange five and six hundred feet long against the blue sky, rolling and crashing through the treetops like fire dragons.

We split off into teams, and I went with Travis Carter, who was known to be a good sawyer—that is, good with a chainsaw. Andrew Ashcraft was his swamper, and I would help Andrew out. We started to cut a fire line, our chainsaws buzzing and revving as we went indirect to the fire—cutting line around the fire and then burning out that section of forest, which robs the fire of fuel. When I wasn't helping the swamper, I was cutting through the thick brush with my Pulaski and the dig team.

We started our burn with our drip torches, the first burn I'd ever witnessed. The brush went right up, *WHOOOOSH*. The temperature out there was hovering near a hundred degrees, and the radiant heat from the flames made it even hotter. I was sweating buckets under my yellows, and the odd feeling came back again. A strange, disembodied, out-of-body feeling, as if my mind were floating away from my skull and riding the wind.

I know this feeling, I thought as I slammed the Pulaski into the base of a thick shrub. *Where have I felt this before?*

Then it hit me. At parties. When I was on X.

I began to panic. Something in my body was releasing Ecstasy into my bloodstream when I was supposed to be fighting a fire. I felt like my head was expanding and getting lighter. I was rolling for sure.

"*I'mgonnadie I'mgonnadie I'mgonnadie,*" I muttered. I broke out in a cold sweat. I looked down at my hands and they seemed to be two miles away, attached to some other body.

Shut the fuck up, I said to myself. *Keep your head down. These guys will get you through it.*

I could think of only one possibility: I'd done so many drugs in the past that some of their residue had been stored in my muscle tissue. Now that I was working and sweating and testing my body to the limit, those chemicals were being released.

Maybe there was fear in there, too. And self-doubt. I'd never been to a place so remote and forbidding. What if I failed my brothers? What if I let them down?

I worked in a daze for hours with one hour-long break for lunch. I managed to make it through the day and we stopped the fire from spreading into our sector. I missed my family. I missed Michaela. And I was scared someone would look in my eyes and say, "Are you fucking tripping out here, Donut?"

As we walked back, I heard and saw animals fleeing the fire. Most of the wildlife had gotten out when they smelled the first whiffs of smoke, but a few were still left. I saw a pack of rabbits, their paws singed from the burning brush, rushing through the undergrowth. I thought, *I'm just as scared as they are.*

I was zombified, totally spent. Chris was behind me on the hike back to camp, and he was fuming. "Move your ass!" he was shouting. Finally I saw one of the other hot-shots, Boone McCarty, come back toward us. He had a concerned look on his face. He pulled Chris out of the line and I could hear them having a conversation. I didn't know what it was about, but I guessed it was about me.

Later, I found out that Boone had told Chris there was a fine line between motivating the rookies and abusing them. Chris laid off for a while.

When we got back to our camping site, I sacked out. I was so exhausted that all I had time to do was take off my boots and get into my sleeping bag before I blacked out. And then the coughing started. My allergies kicked in and I was coughing up a storm. My body was sick. It was like I was going through withdrawal.

But from what? The last time I'd done heroin was about a month before.

The trip was doing strange things to me. My body cramped up so bad I cried in my sleeping bag. I tried to stifle the sobs. I got out of the bag and started slamming my fist into my thighs, trying to get them to unclench.

I hardly slept the whole night, and I watched the sun coming up through the pines, miserable and thoroughly spent. But we had to go back to the line. Eric was getting updates on the radio and we hoped the fire had lain down overnight. No such luck. We ate a breakfast of Frosted Flakes and tramped back to the fire.

It was another horrible day. Even the intense training we'd been through hadn't prepared me for sixteen hours of all-out effort. I found myself on the edge of blacking out. And the fire seemed too enormous to even conceive of. How do you stop something that big with an ax and some saws?

That night Eric came up to me as I was eating. Even if

you did something stupid or lazy, Eric never yelled. He was quiet, and some of the guys who went before me mistook that for his being standoffish or distant. Like he didn't care. But he did. He just gave you this look, a look of disappointment that sank right into you.

He didn't look disappointed now, just concerned.

"Hey, Donut."

"Yup?"

"I didn't get much sleep last night with you hacking. You okay?"

"Yes, sir," I said. That was a lie.

"Maybe you should find a spot farther away from the guys so you don't keep them awake all night."

"Got it."

Eric wasn't being a dick; he just needed the crew to sleep.

Boone McCarty heard us talking. After Eric left, he came up to me. "Why don't you stay in the medical tent?"

I nodded, but by now I was paranoid. I thought Boone was testing me, trying to get me to quit for medical reasons. The worst thing you can be on a fire line out in the wilderness is a liability. Even if you're not kicking ass as a hotshot, you cannot be a burden on your brothers. I felt like I'd come out to Chiricahua to prove myself and get my respect and I was blowing it.

"Yes, sir," I said. But instead, I dug into my pack and found some NyQuil.

This'll do it, I thought. *Knock me right out*. I unscrewed the cap and glugged the nasty liquid. But in my eagerness to get some sleep, I overdid it. I drank most of the bottle before passing out.

Later, I realized Boone was just worried about me.

I threw up once in the middle of the night—on all

fours—but at least I slept. I woke up to the sound of men screaming at me.

"Shut that fucking thing off!"

What were they talking about? I heard music and someone singing. Something about hats and clothes and what you want.

Oh God. It was "Tie Me Down," the song that acted as my cell phone alarm. I'd taken so much NyQuil that I'd slept through it. Twice. I grabbed my phone and thumbed the volume down. The boys were not pleased.

That day I was out on the line with Boone. We were walking down a dirt road, the fire roaring off to the left.

"I'm going interior," Boone said.

"Okay," I said.

He turned away and headed toward the tree line.

"Wait! What does that mean?"

Boone shook his head.

"I'm going *that* way"—he pointed into a stand of tall pine—"to burn some. We need to get some heat established in there, suck the fire away from the road."

That was the first time I realized that hotshots actually shaped wildfires. They cut lines to stop them and started blazes to suck energy away from the places they wanted to protect.

I gave Boone the thumbs-up. He unslung his torch, and ten seconds later he'd disappeared into the brush and I was left standing on the road.

Boone knows how to lead the fire with his drip torch, I thought, *like getting a dog to follow you by dangling a steak in your hand. Just by listening, he knows where the fire is going.*

I listened. All I could hear was the sound of wind followed by a crunching roar. Every time the fire hit a pine tree and ate through the dry needles, it made a sharp swirling sound, like an animal clicking its tongue in its throat.

I couldn't make any sense out of it. I didn't know if the fire was coming toward me or heading west. I caught a glimpse of Boone setting fire to the forest floor, and then he disappeared again.

The rolling from the Molly had subsided somewhat, but now it was replaced with fear. *If Boone calls on the radio and says he's hurt, you have to go in there*, I thought. But I was sure I'd run into the path of the fire like a dumb fuck and get burned up before I was ten feet in. *Damndamndamn this is nuts. This is nuuuuuuts...*

The radio was silent. Ten minutes later—though it felt like an hour—Boone walked out and nodded to me. His face was blackened by smoke. He acted like he'd just gone to 7-Eleven for a Slurpee.

I was trying to learn the job, watching and listening. That week on the line, with my body still feeling bizarre, I listened to Eric brief us about an upcoming burn. We would use our drip torches on a stand of trees that rode up a mountain and down the other side.

That's like fifty thousand acres, I said to myself. *What the fuck are we doing?* Later I would come to realize we were burning fifty thousand acres so that we could save five hundred thousand.

I was in awe. We were specks in these hundreds of thousands of acres. Yet we were in control of them. We were like gods, deciding which parts of the forest would live and which would die. And there was no one to tell us "Stop!"

Later that week on the fire, the fire got so bad that Eric told us that we had to work through the night and the entire next day. A thirty-two-hour shift. Otherwise, the thing was going to get away from us and burn up half of southwest Arizona. We couldn't have that.

The teams headed indirect to the fire. A few teams were cutting and swamping brush, others were digging with their Pulaskis, and a couple of guys were scouting ahead, looking for the next firebreak or acting as lookouts. That day, Travis Carter, Andrew, and I were clearing a firebreak along with three other sawyer teams. The fire was off to our west, and I could see it eat through the tops of pines, which seemed to dance, swaying back and forth as the flames consumed them. Maybe it was the heat haze. Or maybe it was my brain.

Smoke filled my nostrils and my lungs itched. I felt like a robot. The muscles around my shoulders were two knots as I swung the Pulaski. I began to lose track of time. My vision was covered in blackness.

"Hey, Donut!"

I snapped back.

"Donut!" It was Travis.

"Yeah?" I said.

"What's up with you?"

"I'm good, bro."

Please just let me make it through this, I pleaded with God. *Don't let me fail in front of my brothers.*

It was as if my partying days were trying to pull me back. They were getting revenge on me for abandoning them. There were times I wanted to black out, to drop down onto the dry brush and be carried to the medical tent and then choppered out.

You ain't got what it takes, I said to myself. *These guys are hotshots. You're a tweaker.*

With a different crew, I might have bugged out completely and given up. But Granite Mountain was a family, and I could tell that the guys were starting to warm up to me. That night, though I was still sick as a dog, I was picked for a food challenge. This was part of the initiation process: making rookies compete to see who could eat the most of a chosen type of food. That time, the selection was Frosted Flakes. I downed eight boxes before my stomach clenched up. The other guys thought I couldn't eat any more because I was skinny. But it was also because I was drug-sick.

"You almost had it!" Travis said as I admitted defeat. The boys were gathered around me, slapping me on the back and laughing. It felt good.

No way was I going to let them down.

CHAPTER THIRTEEN

We worked the fire for two weeks, the maximum allowed. We dug firebreaks and cut tons of brush and we held the line against the fire.

I began to realize that my fears about the veterans were misguided. During training, they'd made every attempt to find out what made me tick. They really wanted to learn who I was. I'd worried they'd done that so they could break me when the moment was right. Expose me. But I was wrong. That wasn't their intention at all.

Guys covered for each other all the time. Travis Turbyfill was one example. He was an ex-marine who could do just about everything. If we needed to modify one of the buggies to carry a special piece of equipment, we went looking for him. He fixed and modified our tools. Communications equipment, too—Travis had hucked a radio all over for the marines, so some days you'd come back from the fire line and find him with all the parts of our radio spread out over a blanket as he patiently put it together.

But while serving, Travis had suffered a serious head injury. A training exercise was what I heard, but I never talked to him about it. People's pasts were their own: If you wanted to talk about it, that was your call. If not, we respected that.

That head injury had left Travis with a strange symptom: lack of balance. Maybe his inner ear thingy had gotten knocked out of whack, but if you just looked at the man wrong, he'd fall over. If we were in camp and we heard a thump, we'd call out, "Travis, you all right, dude?" Howling with laughter.

But if we were on the trail, especially with a drop to one side, the guy behind Travis would keep close to him. Nobody had to say anything, it was just something we became aware of and all took as part of our duty.

I started to get to know the guys. I was still in awe of Eric. Was there anything the motherfucker couldn't do? Ice climber, surfer, mountain biker, *and* a college grad. Being so calm and so even-keeled, though, he had a weakness for goofballs like me. I made it my mission to crack that man up every chance I got. I'd play some hard-core techno and start dancing like I was back at a rave.

"Hey, Eric, check this shit out!"

He'd look at me, take a sip of coffee out of his camp cup, and just shake his head.

Jesse Steed was a full-on meathead. Ex-marine, super into fitness, really good with a chainsaw. If you got past his leatherneck stuff, he was a teddy bear.

Robert Caldwell didn't look like a hotshot. He was balding at twenty-one. Looked like he was going to ask you if he could do your taxes. But his famous quote to us was: "I'd rather die in my boots than live in a suit." He had a weird strength. We weighed the same, but he'd disappear down the trail ahead of me quicker than a gazelle being chased.

One day we were walking in to a fire and Robert went past me with a chainsaw on his shoulder. I looked over and he had a cigarette in his mouth underneath his mustache.

"Are you serious? You're gonna kick my ass on the trail *and* smoke?"

He grinned at me.

If you looked at Clayton Whitted, you'd think he was a truck driver or a former college tight end. Big dude, big smile. But Clayton was a man of God. He was the real deal, a Christian through and through. He always had his Bible with him, and back in Prescott, he worked as a youth minister. Led Bible classes.

I wanted to be like that. But not yet. I was only nineteen.

But if you had any spiritual questions, Clayton was the guy to see. He seemed to know what to do with his life, had that focus that I was looking for. Sometimes it got him in trouble. There was a story I heard pretty quickly about Clayton and another hotshot working on cutting a big-ass tree out of the fire line. The roots went deep, and neither of them noticed how close the fire was until their backpacks started smoking and lighting up. Clayton calmly turned, grabbed the packs, threw them to safety, then turned back to see the tree falling right at him. He stepped out of the way and the thing came down—*WHOMMMMP!*—right where he'd been standing. Clayton carried on like nothing happened.

The fittest dude on the crew was Travis Carter. He'd grown up on a ranch outside of Yarnell. Quiet as all get out. But the man was half cyborg. He'd get up in the morning, go to CrossFit, do their insane workout, show up to work, rip on a 'saw all day, then hit CrossFit again on his way home to his wife and two young kids. He'd say two words the whole day, but he could serve up anyone on Granite Mountain.

I'd spent most of my teenage years around guys whose main ambition was to score some primo weed and tasty nachos, all on the same night. Just being around Granite Mountain expanded my horizons.

I didn't like everyone at first. Later on in my career, Billy Warneke joined the crew, and he was one of the ones I didn't get along with right away. He just rubbed me the wrong way somehow—it was almost a chemical response. During PT, he'd be trailing me during our hikes, mile after mile with this blank expression on his face, and I'd be like, *Go ahead and pass my struggling ass, damn it,* but he never would. Then one day we were out on a fire and he was carrying someone's pack who was feeling sick that day. Did it without being asked. On top of that, he was a badass ex-marine, and I respected that. I went over and started talking to him that day and learned that he was expecting his first child. A girl.

We had a resident thug-life character, Anthony Rose, who joined up in 2012. Originally from Chicago, he tried to play it like he was a gangster. Then his girlfriend would call and he'd turn into a proper gentleman on the phone, while we wilded out in the background. A hard worker. Smart as hell. Baby on the way, too.

What did we have in common? We'd all been down different roads searching for a decent life. Some had become drug fiends for a while; some had tried the military and seen things they couldn't unsee. But most of us had found what we wanted in Granite Mountain. A steady job. Service. Adventure.

I was learning the job. A few days into the Chiricahua

fire, the boys let me do the weather. Out in the wilderness, weather and fuel are what drives a fire. To know how a fire might act in the next ten minutes, you need to get extremely localized conditions, so a few of us carried a belt weather kit in a little pouch. In each kit are a sling psychrometer for measuring humidity, an anemometer for measuring wind speed, a small bottle of distilled water, and a compass.

The psychrometer is the most important tool. It has two parts: a wet-bulb thermometer and a dry-bulb. You find a spot typical to the terrain and the fuels that are burning nearby. You stand in a shady spot (or block the sun with your body if there's no shade) so that the radiant heat doesn't affect the reading. Then you dab some of the distilled water on a wick attached to the wet bulb, let the bulb down on the metal chain it's attached to, and start swinging it in a tight circle. You face into the wind so your body temperature isn't throwing off the reading and you swing for a full minute. Check the temperature, taking care not to put your finger on the glass. Swing again. After a minute, check. If the temperature hasn't changed, you have your wet-bulb reading. Then you look at the dry bulb and get a number. With those two readings and the humidity chart you carry on a piece of laminated paper, the psychrometer will tell you what the humidity in the air is. Then you check the wind speed and direction.

You check the weather every hour. If the conditions are changing fast, you reduce that to every thirty minutes. Then you get on the radio frequency the crew is using and say, "Granite Mountain, stand by for weather." You pause a minute to give anyone who wants to write the stats down a minute to whip out their pens and paper. Back on the radio: "At oh one hundred, temp is ninety-six degrees, up two degrees over the last hour. Humidity is fourteen percent, down three. Wind is twelve miles an hour from the south-southwest. Anyone need a repeat?"

The man doing the weather is on the lookout for invisible things. He's watching his brothers' backs for the storm winds that can drive a fire at fifty miles an hour and engulf them in a wall of flame. He's key to keeping everyone alive. The fact that Eric let me do it meant a lot to me.

Toward the end of the roll at Chiricahua, we were being rotated back down the mountain for some sleep and a shower. We'd just finished a thirty-two-hour shift and I was clean worn out. As we were getting ready for the chopper, I felt relief flow through me. I saw Chris looking at me strangely. Chris, my old tormentor, my number one nemesis. He hadn't said much to me on the trip.

"Where's your chin strap, rook?" he yelled.

I felt under my hard hat. Damn it. The plastic chin strap—I could have sworn it had been there this morning. Now it was gone.

"Fuck," I said.

"Can't get on the chopper without a strap," Chris said. I saw a gleam in his eyes. Was he happy I'd fucked up at last?

"Are you fucking kidding me?"

The guys around me shook their heads. We heard the chopper in the distance, making that *whomp-whomp-whomp* noise.

"What should I do?" I yelled.

Chris frowned. "Tell you what. I'll fix you up. Shut your eyes."

I closed them and heard a tearing sound. Something pressed against my helmet and I felt something sticky hit my chin, then wrap around. More tearing sounds. I felt grateful; Chris was looking out for me, showing me some respect.

Finally, the tearing sound stopped. I opened my eyes and Chris was backing away, a smile on his face.

"Thanks, man!" I called out.

"Oh, you're welcome, dude."

Chris started laughing hysterically. The other guys were hacking up a lung as well, even Eric. Someone took a pic with his cell phone and handed it to me. Chris had used about half a roll of fiber tape to attach the helmet. I looked like a total dork with a hard hat taped to his head.

I found out later that Chris had stolen the strap so he could fuck with me. Didn't matter. I was smiling ear to ear. In hotshot crews, you only torture the ones you love.

Leaning back against the vibrating seat in the chopper, I felt I'd achieved something: I'd helped save thousands of acres of God's green earth for bears, mountain lions, rabbits, and red-winged blackbirds. I'd withstood the last traces of drugs in my body. And I'd proved to the nineteen men around me that I wouldn't give up on them, no matter what.

I was part of the brotherhood.

CHAPTER FOURTEEN

If we weren't called to a wildfire, my normal day went like this: Show up at the station at about 7:40 a.m., dressed in my green fire pants, a T-shirt, boots, and a hat. Grab a water (everyone else drank coffee), get my lunch together, sit on the front porch, put a chew in, and shoot the shit with the other guys. At 8:00, we'd have a morning briefing on fire conditions, weather, and JAH, or job analysis hazards, meaning what might kill us out there (falling trees, lightning storms, and a bunch of other dangerous shit). We'd load up and do PT. I'd be nervous as hell, because whether I could make it to the end of a hike was always an open question.

Come back, do solid core body work. A pyramid of pullups, which means you do one, come all the way down, then do two, come all the way down, until you get to ten. Then you count back all the way down to one. By the end, you'd do a hundred pull-ups. Or planks. Or push-ups.

Break for lunch. Then go out and do fuels work around Prescott. Drive to different locations in town and cut brush, make the houses defensible. Three or four hours of that, then head back to the station, clean the saws, wash out the trucks. Final meeting with Eric, where he reviewed our performance.

It was grueling. We'd be out on the trail and someone would look up at the sky and say, "For God's sake, someone start a fire!" Or another guy would call out, "Where's the lightning when you need it?" We wanted to fight fires, not only because that's what we'd been trained to a fine edge to do, but because Eric's training was such a killer.

Fires also meant overtime. There were part-time guys on the crew making twelve or fourteen dollars an hour. They really loved the job, but the money was hard to justify with two or three kids at home. Fires were the only way they could make a decent living. So, in a way, you prayed for the thing you feared.

We didn't turn down fires. You want us in Oregon, Florida, Hawaii? We're there.

In the beginning of a season, we'd do an overnighter. Head out to a mountain that had been flagged and fight an imaginary fire to keep sharp. Spend the night out there and tell some stories and laugh some.

But if there was a fire, we'd be out in the bush. Sometimes we were even sent out to New Mexico or other hotspots and "pre-positioned," staged into an area where there was a high likelihood of flames touching off or lightning strikes. And that summer, the fires were unrelenting. One after the other: Yuma, Chiricahua, southern Arizona. I'd end up putting in 1,100 hours of overtime that season.

I loved what I was doing. Every fire, I learned something different. I learned how to read terrain and how to use a compass to navigate trackless forests. I got better at predicting the weather. I learned basic medical techniques, because if you get hurt on the fire line in the wild, you're likely to die. The work sites can be so remote a chopper could take hours to get you to a hospital.

I started to learn about the different kinds of wildfires. Grass fires, for example, are fast and dangerous. A tall grass fire is a killer. It moves quicker than any other type. If a good wind gets behind it, you'd better pray the wind doesn't shift, because if it does, and you're caught in the green—unburned terrain—that fire is going to run you down. The only good thing about grass blazes is that they tend to die down at night, so you can sneak around them and cut them off before they get going again in the morning.

Big timber is another thing altogether. A fire going through a wilderness with tall pine and sycamore will "crown": It'll fly across the treetops, moving so fast it doesn't even touch the timber, just burning up the needles and leaves as it speeds a hundred feet above your head. In a crowning fire, the flames are almost your second-most-dangerous adversary. It's the trees themselves that'll kill you. You're working ahead of the fire, cutting through pines that are two and three times as thick as your own torso. Mistakes are easy to make. Guys have lost their legs or had their heads caved in.

I started looking at different types of vegetation as fuel and learning their characteristics. Juniper is spread across the Southwest and we often found ourselves fighting blazes where it was the majority of the fuel. It's dry and dusty and especially dangerous because it tends to throw spot fires. Scrub oak will spot less, but it burns super hot. And when you go out into the forest to fight a fire, you have to be aware of what animals like to hide in scrub oak: not only wild turkey and mule deer, but black bear.

Manzanita ("little apple" in Spanish) is an evergreen hardwood that seems to burn forever; the oils stored deep within the plant sustain blazes long after you think they're dead. Trees that carry a lot of oil or resin (pine is one example) will burn faster than hardwoods like maple or cherry. That's why the fatwood you may use to light your fire comes from the heart of a pine—it's packed with resin. The only good thing about manzanita is that if you get poison ivy out in the field, you can use the tree's berries to treat it.

Scrub, brush, and trees react to the radiant heat of the sun. A shrub or a tree can hold three times its weight in moisture. When a fire hits a plant like that, it barely burns (think of green wood smoking and not catching in your fireplace). When temperatures increase, plants release moisture. A piece of timber or brush that experiences a high, dry heat will go from having 300 percent moisture to 30 percent fairly quickly. That number fluctuates more than you would think—a hot sun with low relative humidity can dry out a shrub quick. That's why hotshots take weather measurements each hour. You're measuring how dry the fuel around you is, and that can fluctuate significantly over the course of sixty minutes.

When the plant gets hotter, the fuel becomes easier to ignite. That's why the afternoon hours—when temperatures peak—are the most dangerous ones for wildland firefighters. At night, fires often go to sleep, but between noon and five p.m. is when you really earn your money.

You would think the high desert would have little to burn, but in fact everything in it is flammable. Even cactus catches fire. I never knew that until I became a hotshot. Those things will light up like a green cigar.

Guys told me stories of what to watch out for in the field.

The season before, another crew Chris had been working with was doing fuels work in California in winter, when the temps are cooler and the wind isn't as strong. It's supposed to be easy, a way to rest up and get some hours in before the summer kicks off. But that winter was different. The temperatures were so high that helicopters were flying ice in just to cool the guys down. They were ferrying heatstroke victims out. "Tits up" is the technical term we used to describe heatstroke: You're dehydrated, you're exhausted, your muscles are cramping.

"I thought I'd die of dehydration," Chris told me about that trip. I thought he was joking, but it's true—hotshots have actually died from lack of water out in the field. If you're working a blaze and you get so into it that you forget to hydrate, you can do yourself in. To guard against that, I ended up getting a CamelBak, which is a hydration pack filled with water that you wear like a backpack. That thing saved my ass multiple times.

There are lots of weird ways to die on a job. When you're working big timber, you have to watch out for widowmakers. Those are the things up in the canopy that can come down and kill you. Dead branches, trees, even pinecones—I learned that there are pinecones in the California forest that are big enough to split your skull open.

One time, after we'd worked a thirty-two-hour shift and gotten flown off a mountain, Eric was leading us toward our camp so we could get some sleep. We were marching along the trail, and Eric told us to watch out for widowmakers. I was half-delirious by that time and completely misheard him. I thought he said "spider widow webs." Don't ask me how, that's just what I heard.

"Eric!" I called back.

"Yeah?"

"Just take a rake and rake that shit up!"

I was talking about getting the spiderwebs out of the branches so a black widow wouldn't drop down my neck and bite me.

Eric was confused. "What did you just say, Donut?"

"Get a rake and rake 'em up!"

"What are you talking about, son?" Eric said in his drawl. "*Widowmakers*, Donut. The stuff in the trees. That's what I'm talking about."

I got shit about that for a year. Jesse or Eric would be finishing up a safety briefing and ask for any questions and someone would raise a hand and say, "Sounds good, but when do we get the rakes to rake that shit up?" Guffaws.

There were other things out in the wild to be scared of. Lightning storms were terrifying. We'd be on the slope of mountain ranges and a storm cell would come over and start shooting high electricity down into the pines. The tallest trees acted like magnets for lightning. Then the chaotic winds of the thunderstorm that followed played havoc with the fire itself, driving it one way or another like a dog gone crazy with rabies. Totally unpredictable. A lot of times, if a storm moved in, we pulled back from the fire line, because the chance of getting caught in a shifting blaze was that much higher.

During those times, you'd run out of the tree cover and crouch in a clearing, praying for the lightning strikes to stay away. The rain and hail would be pelting you and freezing you to the marrow. Freezing cold rain running down your back into your underwear. Boy, that was an experience I could have happily missed.

Snakes were another job hazard. A lot of the terrain we

were working in was the natural habitat for speckled rattlers, western diamondbacks, sidewinders, copperheads, and a bunch of other nasty critters. The main reason we wear high leather boots is the smoking debris we walk through, but another good one is to avoid snakebites.

I killed my share. We even had rock parties. When we spotted a big poisonous critter in the area we were working, we'd all grab a rock and have at it. One time we were hiking through a salt cedar swamp. I was trailing behind and all of a sudden I heard someone screaming. "Snake! *SNAKE!*"

"What the hell?" I said to myself.

The hotshot doing the screaming was Mondo, who was famous for his glossy black mustache. As he walked through the salt cedar, a baby rattler had dropped from the tree branches onto him. It was now wriggling on his chest strap. A baby rattler can't control its venom like an adult snake can. It can give you ten times a fatal dose in one of its bites, making it far more dangerous than a grown-up rattler.

We circled around Mondo, wondering what to do. We couldn't smash the damn thing or try to slap it off, for fear that it might strike and kill this guy with one bite to the chest. So we tried to calm him down as the thing wriggled on his shirt. His face was as pale as a sheet of paper.

Finally it dropped off. Mondo sat down, his chest heaving. It took him ten minutes to get calm enough to recover and get back on the trail.

Lizards were a different story. I loved the things. I'd find one on the first day or two of a fire and keep him as a pet, giving him little pieces of my rations to eat. I'd put one in my pocket and he'd just chill in there as I dug line. Let him out back in camp and let him crawl over me as I started to fall asleep. I even talked to the little guys. Why not? It's just you and nineteen of your best friends. No one out here to judge you.

A bunch of the guys adopted little friends for our excursions. Crawdads, which are little crustaceans that look like mini lobsters, were a favorite. Guys would carry them around in little jars of water attached to their belt loops and then set them free when we left. Out on the fire line, you could get to feel like a machine working in a smoky, noisy, dangerous factory. Why not have a little buddy to call your own?

Don't knock it if you haven't tried it.

I'd expected dangerous animals as part of the job. If your workplace is the wild, you have to accept that. But what I didn't foresee was the cartels.

Some of the fires we fought were in forests or mountain ranges that extended all the way down into Mexico. We were cutting brush and digging fire lines along well-known drug routes, and you had to be on your toes or you could find yourself with a nice neat hole in your head. The cartels ran drugs and illegal immigrants up and down the same trails we were using to reach the fire line. And often, they didn't know we were coming.

Sometimes they even started fires to cover up their activities, whether it was smuggling desperate people across the border or moving bales of marijuana along the trails. The La Brea Fire in 2009 near Santa Barbara was caused by drug traffickers who were using some kind of cooking device. One hundred thirty-seven square miles of prime ranchland was turned into cinders. After hotshots went in and knocked the fire down, at the risk of their own lives, investigators traced the blaze to a remote little canyon in the Los Padres National Forest. Near the origin spot, they found an AK-47, charred to shit, and about thirty thousand marijuana plants.

Maybe the traffickers were cooking up their dinner as they watched over the plants when the fire started. Maybe they were getting some shut-eye and a spark from their campfire touched off a propane tank. Or maybe they were camped on a rival's territory and they ignored the orders to leave, so someone got to them and burned their crop.

In 2011, the year I joined up, the Monument Fire erupted in eastern Arizona. It burned up about thirty thousand acres. Investigators traced the origin to the Coronado National Forest, which was closed to visitors and vehicles. The only people operating in Coronado were the cartels and drug traffickers. The cartels employ scouts to watch the trails for Border Patrol and rival gangs. Sometimes they light signal fires to let people know their sector is too dangerous for cartel soldiers. Or, at night, they get cold and they start a campfire to keep warm.

Two other fires burning at the same time—including one that burned over eight hundred square miles—were also started by humans. These were most likely not innocent mistakes. Cartels use fire as a weapon. If the authorities are busy fighting a raging wildfire, they have no resources to catch bandits or snakeheads, the guides who brought the illegal immigrants across the border.

A lot of the pot farms have armed guards. Other times the cartels leave the farms unguarded but will set traps— wire strung up across the road that can decapitate you if you're driving in a UTV, or trip wires laid on the trails and attached to loaded shotguns or IEDs. We had to watch out for all of that shit.

One time we went out to the Arizona-Mexico border to

fight a wildfire, and at the briefing, Eric paused and then said something I'd never heard before: "I want you guys to wear your yellows at all times. We have information that there are two cartels battling it out on the terrain we'll be going into. There are reports they have high-powered rifles. And I've also been told that they know we're coming in and, so long as we identify ourselves in our yellows, we'll be left alone to fight the fire."

Whaaaaat? This was some cloak-and-dagger stuff.

We went out into the brush line and started cutting. There was extra tension in the crew, just wondering if we were being watched. It's a spooky feeling, gives you an icy patch at the base of your spine.

We didn't get shot at on that job, but we did find a Mexican dude nearly dead of thirst on the side of the road. At first we thought he was a corpse. He was just lying there in the morning light, unable to move. We were on our way off the fireline and we said to each other, "What do we do?" Mondo gave him some Gatorade, but he was so messed up he couldn't keep anything down and so dehydrated that an EMT we called to the scene could barely find a vein for an IV. The Border Patrol finally came and took him away.

I'm not sure if he was a cartel soldier or an illegal immigrant who got left behind. But a couple more hours out there alone and he would have been a goner.

Hotshots are at the mercy of the weather and of history. When 9/11 happened and the planes went into the Twin Towers, the FAA shut down all air traffic in the United States. You couldn't even fly a helicopter. A crew of hotshots was working high up in California and they were stranded. They had to hike out some hellacious number of miles. When you're a hotshot, you're an afterthought, invisible to everyone except your family and your brothers. If you're due to rotate off a mountaintop and fog settles in or high wind grounds the choppers, forget it. You walk.

We flew to Montana that summer and fought a big timber blaze. The choppers couldn't come to us—the winds were too extreme. We were worn out after a week of swamping and cutting, cold food, and little sleep. We were like black-faced zombies.

"So what do we do?" I asked Eric.

"We hike out."

Shoot me now, I thought. There were no roads where we were. It was the trackless wilderness. And it was wet; it had been raining on and off for four days. The worst part was our boots. When water gets into them, your feet rub against the leather and they turn to sushi. Just raw, pulverized flesh.

I didn't say a word. This was the job. We hiked out.

CHAPTER FIFTEEN

The thing you look out for as a hotshot, of course, is fire. Hotshots trade stories of ones that got out of control, narrow escapes, legendary fires from the past. I loved to hear about the blazes that went back before our time.

The one that you heard the most about was South Canyon. That was sort of the model of what could go wrong for a wildland firefighter in the Southwest. It had all the elements we saw every day: wind, storm, flame, steep slopes, chaparral. But those elements had come together in a few short minutes and killed fourteen firefighters. Before I joined up, Granite Mountain had even gotten a trip together—called a "staff ride," which all hotshot crews do as part of their training—to go visit Storm King Mountain, where the fire happened, in central Colorado, just to study the terrain and study the decisions those firefighters had made. The Granite Mountain crew wanted to honor their sacrifice by learning from it.

South Canyon began with a drought. On July 2, 1994, after two years of low rainfall, a lightning strike ignited a wildfire near the base of Storm King Mountain, which is part of the Rocky Mountain system. Like many lightning fires, it started high up on a ridge, this time in a thicket of piñon pine and juniper. It was one of forty wildfires set off by dry lightning storms in the span of a few days, and South Canyon was at first thought to be among the minor ones. The terrain was rugged and inaccessible to vehicles and lacked any possible helispot to land a chopper. No hotshots or resources were dedicated to the fight in the first two days, and the fire consumed only three acres. It was skunking along the ridgeline, making the locals nervous but doing little damage.

Left to its own devices, the fire grew. On the morning of July 5, seven firefighters hiked two and a half hours and began cutting a landing area for a helicopter on the steep slope and a firebreak to hold the fire on its southwest flank. An air tanker dropped a load of retardant. The crew worked all day and left in the evening to do maintenance on their chainsaws. They were replaced by eight smokejumpers, who parachuted in from jump planes. The smokejumpers saw that the fire had already slopped over the first fire line cut by the seven firefighters, so they started constructing a second one on the east side of the ridge.

A cold front was brewing not far from the fire zone. On July 5, the National Weather Service issued a red flag warning for the area, which meant ideal conditions for wildland fire combustion had been reached. Low humidity, dry fuel, and high, gusting winds. For the civilian, a red flag warning means "get ready to move."

But the next morning, the meteorologist responsible for warning firefighters on the Colorado blazes about changing conditions realized the front was more powerful than he'd first imagined. It was carrying gusts of up to forty miles per

Eric Marsh, Jesse Steed, Boone McCarty, and other Granite Mountain hotshots formulating a plan at the Whitewater Baldy fire.

A catwalk in New Mexico. Granite Mountain was tasked with taking much of it down, due to possible flooding.

Hiking to the fireline with my brothers: Left to right: Me, Bob Caldwell, Philip Maldonado, and Clayton Whitted.

Hiking out of Montana where no choppers were available. Andrew Ashcraft collected flowers for his wife close to this spot.

Clayton Whitted making the crew laugh with his shenanigans.

Anthony Rose his rookie year. He painted a soot heart on his face after losing a bet with me.

Eating MREs in Montana, far from civilization, with Jesse Steed and Eric Marsh.

The famous giant juniper tree that we saved during the Doce Fire in Prescott, Arizona.

Garret Zuppiger burning brush in Nevada. That was one of the largest fires I was ever on—roughly 500,000 acres.

The Thompson Ridge Fire in New Mexico. Repositioning a huge log so we can cut it apart.

The Doce Fire in Prescott, showing the burned areas.

In front of Prescott Fire Station 71, where I did my Fire Explorers training as a kid, with some of the items dropped off by local citizens. *Photo by Wade M. Ward.*

The procession to recover my brothers, with hundreds of firefighters, policemen, and other supporters. It felt like the day Arizona stood still. *Photo by Wade M. Ward.*

Former Granite Mountain hotshots taking in the memorial, with pictures and pieces of wildland firefighting gear. *Photo by Wade M. Ward.*

Here I am shaking hands with Harold Schaitberger, the president of the International Association of Firefighters. Vice President Joe Biden is in the background. *Photo by Wade M. Ward.*

Reading the Hotshot's Prayer in front of a packed stadium in Prescott Valley, Arizona, with the nation and world watching. *Photo by Wade M. Ward.*

hour. The winds could roll over a fire and blow it up without any advance warning. The firefighters needed to know that the weather situation was becoming potentially hazardous. The meteorologist got on the phone and made a series of urgent calls to different dispatchers. When he called Grand Junction District, which was overseeing the South Canyon Fire, they thanked him and promised to get the news out.

But the channels were bristling with updates from various crews and officials. The message was lost in the rush and never broadcast to the men and women on the ridge. Supervisors knew a cold front was moving toward them, but not its severity.

The smokejumpers had to break off around midnight on July 5 when boulders started rolling down from the top of the ridge, big enough to kill you if one caught you in the head. On the morning of July 6, the original crew and a new set of smokejumpers were joined by twenty hotshots from a Prineville, Oregon, crew. "What the hell's that?" one of them called when they arrived at the fire around eleven a.m. "You've got to be kidding me. That fire's dead!"

The firefighters began building a second helispot and cutting firebreaks. Most of them were working in a descending line across the western flank of the ridge, in dense brush that at some points grew above their head to twelve feet—so thick that the men and women couldn't even see the bottom of the ridge. The firefighters were isolated, cocooned in a thin corridor between tall stands of oak brush. They didn't have eyes on the fire, and no lookout had been posted to keep a good eye on the mountain. But they knew the basic rule that all firefighters learn: Don't let a fire get below you on a slope. The reason is simple: A wildfire moves much faster upslope than down. The terrific heat flowing in front of the fire precooks the trees and brush while raising the ambient temperature. This can cause the terrain to burst into flame even before the fire reaches it. Crowning fires have been measured moving upslope at one hundred miles per hour.

Some of the smokejumpers were nervous. They were deep in the green in front of a burning fire. "Hey," some of the men called to their supervisor, "we shouldn't be here." But none of them pressed the issue. "It's that fine line between bringing up concerns and being a whiner," said one firefighter after the tragedy.

The fire that had started on the ridge had burned down to the drainage below, to the west of the firefighters. There were stands of Gambel oak and oak brush on the slope that had lost their twigs and leaves to the fire, but the trunks and branches—dry as tinder—remained.

Early in the afternoon, the foreman of the Oregon hotshots felt the wind shift and reported that the breeze had turned "squirrely." The fire was still growing, now covering 127 acres. But it was one among many blazes ripping their way across central and western Colorado. The crews were several hundred yards below the top of the ridge. The bottom of the western drainage, a gully filled with brush that was, in spots, less dense than the hillside, was their escape route.

The oak was dense. The hotshots and smokejumpers had to cut spaces into the vegetation just to dispose of the cut brush. Helicopters were dumping water on hot spots from buckets extended from their bellies.

The fire entered the afternoon hours, when temperatures are hottest and wildfires are most dangerous. Later, officials would set the chances of an ember combusting a leaf or a twig on contact at 90 to 100 percent. Humidity was low, temperatures were high, the fuel was bone dry. There was only one missing element for a firestorm: wind.

Some of the smokejumpers could see down to the bottom of the gully. There was orange flame eating its way through the oak brush, and burning pinecones and branches were rolling down into the foliage. "You know what it's going to do?" one of them said to his partner. "It's going to back down into this draw and come up on this side at us."

"Then why don't we get out of here?" the other fire-fighter said.

There were other fires in history where flames had erupted out of a canyon and caught fleeing firefighters on a hillside, and most firefighters could tell you the details from memory. Mann Gulch stood out on this list. In 1949, in the Gates of the Mountains Wilderness, smokejumpers were walking toward a fire in Mann Gulch when a storm front blew it into a fireball, burning across three thousand acres in ten minutes. The men turned and ran with the fire at their backs, the flames sweeping up a grass-covered slope that angled at thirty-seven degrees. The men threw away their tools and their crosscut saws as they raced toward the ridgeline. The foreman, looking behind to see the flames racing and hearing the rising sound in his ears, took out his matches and lit a fire in the high grass right in front of the crew. He was hoping to create an escape fire that his men could lie down in while the more powerful firestorm swept around them.

But the men charging up behind the foreman refused to enter the escape fire. One cried, "To hell with that!" and the crew raced toward a hogback above them that was covered in boulders and rocks. The foreman lay down in the escape fire and felt the intense updrafts from the firestorm lift him bodily off the ground, not once but several times.

Of the sixteen men who ran for their lives, only three—which included the foreman—escaped.

On Storm King Mountain, at around 3:20 p.m., the dry cold front that the meteorologist had warned dispatchers about arrived at the bottom of the slope. Its winds were gusting to forty-five miles per hour. When the winds hit the blaze at about 4:00 p.m., the fire blew up. It turned eastward and started to run, throwing hundred-foot flames into the sky. It jumped the fire line below the firefighters and began racing up the slope toward them, deafeningly loud. Its flames shot two hundred feet in the air, then three hundred. It was a freight train, and it was unstoppable.

Just like at Mann Gulch, the fire chased the crew, this time across the top of Hell's Gate Ridge. It sucked the oxygen from their mouths and wrapped them in flames as its gases and heat pushed them over the ridgetop and into a canyon on the other side. A helicopter pilot shouted into his radio, but all he heard were a series of clicks. Then a single scream that lasted several seconds before the transmission ended or the radio burned up.

Two other firefighters, who'd been directing helicopters to the second helispot, a short distance from Hell's Gate Ridge, also ran from the burning wall of flame, but their escape path was blocked by a steep, rocky chute fifty feet deep. With nowhere else to go, they plunged down into the narrow canyon. Here the fire overwhelmed them.

Fourteen men and women died on Storm King Mountain. Firefighters from near and far continue to this day to make pilgrimages to Hell's Gate Ridge to see the landscape, to create in their minds a small film of what happened, with the key moments emphasized. They wanted to learn the lessons of South Canyon. Inscribe them in their memories.

If you're not safe, speak your mind.

If a storm is on the way, get the hell away from the fire. Safety first.

CHAPTER SIXTEEN

That summer I saw the full spectrum of hotshottin'. It was a blur of smoke, chaw, exhilaration, being dog-tired—and brotherhood.

I was alive in a way I couldn't remember feeling before. Rejuvenated. I could run for hours now. Not fast, but I could run. I was tanned, my chest had filled out with muscle, my thighs were straining against my jeans, and my eyes were clear.

I was spending half my time in the wilderness. Bald eagles soared over our campsites in the morning. At night, sometimes in temperatures below freezing, we'd sit around roaring fires talking about famous blazes the veteran guys had fought, like the 1990 Dude Fire, which killed six fire-fighters. 122-degree temperatures in the region of this deadly blaze were extreme enough to close the Phoenix air-port, because no one knew if fully loaded airplanes could operate in that kind of heat.

Or we put on skits to entertain ourselves. The wooden handle of the Pulaski became a microphone stand and an ax would become a guitar and guys would sing out into the wilderness, hopelessly out of tune. My big star moment was performing "I'm a Little Teapot." I had one hand on my hip like the handle and the other curved out like the spout, the whole nine yards. The competition was fierce; the prize was a tin of Copenhagen chaw, and we all wanted it bad.

Guys acted out scenes from Granite Mountain's past or imitated each other or Hollywood actors. The dialogue was often unprintable. The winners that day were Brandon Bunch and Boone McCarty, who had done a skit featuring an awesome old-timer named Todd who worked in the Granite Mountain office and did a lot for all of us. Brandon played Todd and Boone pretended to shave him and put a chaw in his mouth, and it was just hilarious. Guys actually fell off their logs laughing. I didn't have a chance.

We were like boys playing in God's country. I grew to love that feeling, of being alone with the night and the firs in our own private part of the wild.

Back in Prescott, I'd see some of my old druggie friends downtown and they'd do a double take. "*Brendan?*"

I had no idea how they'd react to me, whether they'd be cynical or hating on me because I wouldn't snort some heroin for old times' sake. But I got none of that. In fact, my druggie friends were proud of me. Imagine that!

I was like that guy who made it out of Alcatraz. One guy saw me and said, "Dude, even if you begged me for a toke, I wouldn't give it to you. I wish I was doing what you're doing." When they found out I was a father, they were even more stoked. I was their little success story. There weren't too many of those in Prescott that I knew. So they wished me well and I did the same to them.

I didn't miss the drugs, honestly. I never want to go back. I'd found my calling as a hotshot, but my life was far from perfect. I was having problems with Natalie. We were fighting all the time, mostly about Michaela. My grandma had told me once, "Brendan, you're the one who's going to break the cycle in this family." To really stop the cycle of addiction and hopelessness, I knew I had to raise Michaela right. And I couldn't do that alone.

So during lunch breaks, I'd be on the phone going at it with Natalie. I have a temper. I get it from both my parents. And I'd be yelling "bitch" this and "motherfucker" that and be getting it right back from her. One day after I'd put down the phone, Eric came up to me.

"What's going on, Brendan?"

I told him about it. About the fights over how to raise my daughter, custody, the whole ball of wax. I got pissed off all over again talking about it. I told him there were times I felt like getting away from it all, heading home to just be with my daughter.

"So what are you gonna do? Are you gonna go home and blow up at her?"

I cursed a bunch more. Eric shook his head, his kind blue eyes studying me. "Brendan, what else do you have besides this job? If you leave, you're not gonna be able to get another job. You're still on probation. You leave, and Natalie will get full custody and your daughter will grow up barely knowing you."

I nodded. I was a bit shocked by the conversation, actually. No man had ever taken the time to look at my life, analyze my problems, and try to find a way to solve them. I was used to my mom yelling at me about what a fuckup I was. But being rational about how to change? That was brand new to me.

Eric wasn't even a dad, but he taught me how to be one. He taught me about patience and compromise. He had a saying: "If I make you a better firefighter, that's all well and good. But if I don't make you a better man, then I've failed you."

I started listening to Eric. I learned patience. I learned to put myself second. I bit down on the rage and even tried to see things from Natalie's point of view. But most of all, I manned up. And whenever Eric saw me about to lose it again, he'd find me and ask me what was going on. And I'd instantly feel my blood pressure start to drop.

No one had ever done that for me before.

Those first nights I had Michaela as a single dad, I didn't know what the hell I was doing half the time. One night, she was sick as all get out, a fever of 102 and lethargic. She couldn't keep any food down and her head was lolling back like she was a rag doll.

I was terrified. I couldn't call my ex, and my mom was out of town.

I called up Travis Turbyfill, the ex-marine with the balance problem. Travis had two little girls and his wife was a nurse.

He picked up. I launched right into the details, then blurted out, "Dude, what do I do?"

"Calm down, Donut," he said. He told me that first I had to knock down the girl's temperature. Then he instructed me on what medicine to get from CVS. Said to draw a cool bath when I got back. Walked me through the whole thing.

Travis was always talking to me about what he'd learned about being a dad. I remember on the way home from one big fire I was talking in the buggy about everything we'd done that day. I was starting to think like Eric or the other veterans: how to outthink a fire. We hooted and hollered and called each other liars.

I felt good. We'd saved some homes that day. People had come up and thanked us. I was a little high off it.

When we were done bullshitting, Travis smiled at me. "Donut, one thing."

I nodded. "Yeah?"

"When you get home, your brain is going to keep throwing up scenes from the past few days. Your brain doesn't know the fire is over. But you've got to turn that off. Forget the fire. Spend some time with your daughter. Get into her world, man. She doesn't give a shit about hotshots. She cares about you."

It was great advice. And I didn't understand it then, being twenty and, in my own mind, indestructible. But more than one of the dads told me the same thing during that first season. I think what they were saying to me was: Hold your daughter and forget about anchors and chains and all the rest of it. Because this could be the last time you see her.

We were a kind of family. We had barbecues to open the season in May, and then to close it in September. We'd get together at a local park, cook some ribs, throw the Frisbee, meet the families of the other guys, and goof around with their kids. A lot of hotshot crews only spent time together on the job, but Granite Mountain was tight.

One thing you never talked about, though, was the danger of the job. We all knew there were risks, and we talked about the specific things to watch out for. But dying in a fire? We never discussed it. We never talked about how our kids would see the news on TV and be unable to sleep. Or how wives and girlfriends found it hard to let go of us before we flew out to a job.

What, really, could you say?

CHAPTER SEVENTEEN

I was new to the job, but the veteran guys were telling me that it was changing. The *West* was changing. It was getting drier and way more dangerous. I was just too green to know it.

As a hotshot, you see the land up close. Before, I'd drive down the highway and see nothing but the blacktop. But as the weeks went by with Granite Mountain, I started to pay attention to the land. The conditions are like a palm spread out—they can tell your future.

I'd hike into the backcountry and my eye would be scanning the terrain, looking at the color of the vegetation. I noticed that in April, the terrain already looked like high summer. Brown everywhere. Streams that should be three feet wide just a trickle. Bushes not greening out the way they should because they weren't getting enough moisture.

The West is entering a period of unprecedented dryness. The word "megadrought" is coming into common usage, and it's a scary one for firefighters. The less rain that falls on the forests of the Southwest, the more parched the terrain gets. That means more and bigger wildfires. The numbers are sending us a warning. Since the 1970s, the total area burned in the West each year has tripled. The number of fires over ten thousand acres has increased sevenfold. And the acreage that they burn is six times greater. Since 1998, there has been only a single year when there were as few wildfires as in the most active year in the 1970s.

Climate change is increasing both the number and deadliness of wildfires. In 1989, there were about 140 large blazes per year nationwide. Today the number is almost double that. The peak season back then lasted five months. Now it's seven-plus. Increased temperatures, earlier snowpack melt (by a full month), and drier forests are creating these monster blazes called megafires. Some of these infernos can consume nearly an acre of forest *every second*.

Think about that. An acre is about forty-three thousand square feet. Think of an area that size tightly packed with different species of timber and scrub. Then envision a fire coming through so fast that in the blink of an eye everything is charred out and black.

When we fought the fire at Chiricahua, a lot of the veterans, guys who'd fought hundreds of fires, said it was one of the top ten toughest, nastiest blazes they'd faced, not only because of the steep terrain, but because of the speed and intensity of the fire, driven by weather and the dryness of the fuels it was consuming. But what if these monsters become not the exception but the norm? That, for a hotshot, is not a pleasant thought.

These fires are devastating to the Southwest in a bunch of different ways. Most people think that a big fire is a natural event that has some good aspects to it. It clears the land for new growth to spring up and create new forests. But these big fires damage the trees' ability to reproduce. For that to happen, mother trees need to drop their seeds on good ground. (Ponderosa pines, those beautiful tall trees that sometimes look like Christmas trees on stilts, can cast their seeds only about one hundred yards.) When you wipe out an entire section of trees, many times the full forest doesn't come back. Little scrub trees and grass replace the big pines. The forest changes.

Then there's the human element. By that, I mean the houses that we see in the hills and rural areas. There have always been some there, but now there are more of them and they're more expensive. When people move to places like Wyoming or Nevada or Arizona, if they have enough money, they want the forest views. That means that the hills around Prescott and the small towns of Nevada, Montana, and Idaho are chock-full of new and expensive homes inserted right into the wildland. And that affects how we fight a fire. Sometimes we're called in to places like Chiricahua to protect the pristine wilderness. But more and more often, we're going in to save property. Horse farms. Mansions.

A lot of people who come to the West love nature. Just like me, they're converts. They love the sagebrush, the cacti, and the desert foxes, the whole thing. When they get to somewhere like Prescott, they finally get to buy a piece of it. And they feel protective of the natural beauty of the place.

So what happens? They want their home to look like it's part of the landscape. They don't build a defensible fire perimeter around their home, clearing the brush and trees so that a fire will be prevented from approaching their house. Why move to the West and push nature away? People want to be as close to it as possible. And clearing the land and maintaining that perimeter is a hassle.

Believe it or not, when I started telling people that I

was a hotshot, some got mad at me. "Why do you guys go around burning up those beautiful forests?" one guy in Prescott said to me. "Why don't you just let Mother Nature take her course? She's been doing pretty good for millions of years."

These people kill me.

"Listen," I told him. "*I* didn't put your million-dollar home in the middle of the wilderness. *I* didn't call for help when the fire got too close. Maybe if you hadn't built in the hills, I wouldn't be out there risking my life to save your place. If we let Mother Nature take her course, you can kiss your house good-bye."

A lot of people think that stopping a wildfire is no big deal. Call in a few air tankers, and those DC-10s come swooping overhead, their belly-mounted tanks filled with thousands of gallons of water or fire retardant, and boom, no more fire. Hotshots do love to see the tanker flying in. But it doesn't make the fire go away.

These tankers carry a slurry made up of water and fertilizer, mixed in with a red dye that helps firefighters and pilots determine where they've dropped their loads. The slurry comes down and coats the trees and shrubs, making it harder for the fire to come through. But hotshots still have to go in and dig line and cut brush. The tankers can't save the forests by themselves.

There's another problem. Tankers—and the choppers that bring hotshots to fire lines high up in the mountains—are dangerous, and they're expensive. A pilot can only fly a few hundred feet above the ground when he's carrying the slurry. A lot of the time, he's putting the aircraft through severe updrafts and plumes of hot ash rising from the fire. Those plumes cause turbulence. And the pilot is most likely flying an old propeller plane, powered by piston engines and built when Dwight D. Eisenhower was president.

Politicians love to see those gigantic DC-10s fly over the mountaintop and drop a big load of red retardant on a blaze. It shows they're earning their pay (that's why they're referred to as "CNN drops"). But those tankers are often patched together from old military planes that were rescued from aviation boneyards. They're old and they're expensive to maintain.

All this means one thing: crashes. Between 2001 and 2013, a bunch of pilots have died in tanker accidents. Twenty-two, to be exact.

But that's only part of the story. Since the 1994 South Canyon Fire, four hundred wildland firefighters have died in action. And forty thousand homes have been lost. If hotshots were more visible, if we didn't disappear under the canopy of trees and fight fires out of the public eye, more people might know that number. The local people whose houses we save will do anything for us. But to most Americans, we're invisible.

And that's a problem. Because the fires are getting stronger. And that means more wildland firefighters are going to die trying to fight them.

The fires aren't just getting bigger and more frequent, they're getting hotter. Some can burn up to three thousand degrees Fahrenheit, which is hot enough to melt titanium. There's nothing you can do to protect against a fire that hot if it gets close to you.

Hotshots go to work with very little protection. The yellow Nomex shirts we wear (called "yellows") are fire resistant, but they protect you only up to a couple of hundred degrees Fahrenheit. That might be okay for a grease fire in your kitchen, but in a wildfire, it's nothing. I always thought the only protection the Nomex shirts offered was psychological.

In 1957, the U.S. Forest Service reviewed a series of tragic wildfires and came up with a set of guidelines, "Standard Firefighting Orders and 18 Watchout Situations" (called "10 & 18" in the wildland firefighting community). They detail the proper procedures to fight wildfires safely and are to be "applied in all fire situations." They're still in effect today.

Another important safety recommendation is: "Keep one foot in the black, one in the green." The black is the burned-over section of wildland, where the fire has already eaten through its fuel. It's safe. The green is the untouched land, where dry sagebrush and chaparral are waiting to go up. It's not safe. You're always supposed to keep an escape route within reach while fighting the fire.

When I joined Granite Mountain, one of the pieces of gear I received was a fire shelter. It's a tent made out of fire-resistant material that looks like silver tinfoil. And that's what the outer layer is: aluminum foil that's been bonded to silica cloth. The aluminum radiates the heat back away from you, and the silica cloth slows down the remaining heat. There's another layer of foil inside, attached to sheets of fiberglass.

The shelters can deflect 95 percent of a flame's radiant heat, and they're at their best when a fire passes over you. But if the shelters are hit by flames or the gases that race in front of them, it's a different story. They begin to delaminate at 500 degrees and the foil begins melting at 1,200 degrees.

You carry the shelter in a nylon bag in your pack and, if the fire gets too close, you're supposed to clear as much ground around you as you can, scraping any fuel away with your Pulaski. Then the members of the crew form a tight unit if possible, deploy their shelters, and get inside, their feet pointed out toward the fire. You grip the lower edge of the shelter with your hands so smoke and flame can't get through. You turn your face to try to get as close to the ground as possible. That's where the air is coolest.

And then you pray your ass off.

Aside from the Nomex clothing, fire shelters, and our own education and training, there's really nothing else to protect a hotshot. No emergency beacons, no cavalry coming to save the day. Just the hotshot's own intelligence and experience. And his brothers. When we go out on the fireline, we're deeply vulnerable to the flames. Every hotshot knows that.

CHAPTER EIGHTEEN

One morning, we got a call to southern Arizona. A fire was burning out of control in what we call the wildland-urban interface, the point at which the wildlands meet human habitation. We were being called in to save people and their homes.

When we arrived, we pitched right into the fight the first day. But the blaze kicked our ass, plain and simple. It was unstoppable, roaring up and over the sides of hills. And on those hillsides were houses: ramshackle cabins, million-dollar mansions, and everything in between. People were getting burned out.

The fight was more personal here. We were on a quest to save lives and homes. We worked the brush, cutting and swamping, constructing fire lines and trying to rob the blaze of fuel before it reached the condo developments that were all over the hillsides. But it was being driven by strong winds; it was a shifty fire. I swear to God you got to thinking that it was alive, trying to find a way around us so it could feed. We'd get a break cut, and spot fires would appear past our break. New fires would pop up.

It was backbreaking work, sixteen hours straight. I was ready to drop by the end of the second day. We knocked off around eight p.m. and headed back to where we were sleeping that night. We got to camp and were horsing around, trying to cheer each other up after a bitch of a day. We wanted to go home and see our kids. I, as the crew's class clown, was doing some dance moves as I waited for our meals to heat up.

I got a few of the boys laughing.

"Donut," Chris said, "you ain't all there, boy."

"That's all right," I said. "That's just fine. Check this one out." And I went into some techno robot moves. Awkward as hell. I can't really dance. But the boys were loving it.

Finally, the grub was ready. I sat down and rubbed my hands together, ready to dig into my plate. I heard something to my right, at the edge of the camp, and looked over. In the flicker of the campfire, I saw a bunch of people—men and women, even a few children—huddled around wooden picnic tables. They were wearing civilian clothes. The adults weren't hotshots, for sure.

What the hell are they doing out here?, I thought.

I took a bite of the chicken. Delicious. "Hey, Boone," I called. "Who's that?"

He looked over. "Those," he said quietly, "are the people who lost their houses today."

I looked again. These people were homeless because the fire had outwitted us. Because there weren't enough of us, not enough ground resources, tankers, and dozers. Because we'd failed.

I put my plate down. I felt a mixture of anger and shame. I'd lost my appetite. I wanted to go back out to the fire line and start up all over again. We all felt the same way. Those people had nowhere to go and we were sick about it.

What was worse, after we'd finished our dinner, some of the residents came over to talk to us. One older gentleman with a deeply lined face was wearing a blue jacket and some faded jeans. I wondered if they were all the clothes he had. He came over to me and shook my hand, smiling.

"I want to thank you," he said.

I dropped my head.

"Sir, we didn't do anything. We didn't save your house."

His hand gripped mine tighter.

"You tried. Do you know how much that means to us? You tried and we thank you for that."

I spent a few more minutes talking with him. He'd lost everything. He was going to drive out to Tucson to stay with his daughter, then hopefully come back and rebuild. He loved the landscape. He loved the sun in the morning.

It was a good plan. But what if the insurance wasn't as much as it should have been? What if he ran out of time before he got to live in the desert again? Then he was fucked. Game over.

The civilians left and we were standing there with our half-eaten food. Everyone was silent, deep in their own thoughts.

What were we doing out here if we weren't saving people's houses?

I went back to my sleeping bag, unrolled it, took off my boots and my jeans and my yellows, and climbed inside. I felt the tears coming. I knew they would.

I will work harder tomorrow, I thought. *I don't want to meet any more homeless people out here because I got tired or needed some chow. Fuck that.*

I thought of my first real introduction to firefighting, that textbook back in Fire Explorers. That passage that had gotten me excited, something about those men and women who sacrifice their all to protect the lives and homes of their fellow citizens from the ravages of fire.

Were those the words? I couldn't remember exactly. But I felt it was the oath we'd taken, to give our all. And now these people's photo albums and pets and shelter were smoking ruins. I hated that there were people who'd lost everything sleeping out in the open. Their memories, the places where they were going to live out their lives. Gone.

A month later, we were called to New Mexico. A fire had just blown up in a populated area called Ruidoso. It was a typical situation: a nothing fire that became a big one because there were too many blazes to tamp down. It was called the Little Bear Fire.

On June 4, a lightning-sparked fire was spotted on the western slopes of the Sierra Blanca mountains, in the Lincoln National Forest. By June 7, four acres were burning, in dense mixed conifer—pine trees and other species. The Smokey Bear Ranger District sent out a bulletin to local residents that a lightning strike had set some timber ablaze. "Based on fire acreage and conditions, we're not expecting this to be a large, complex fire," the bulletin read. "We'll probably see smoke for a while, but fire behavior is low to moderate."

"Fire behavior" means what the fire is doing. Is it being driven by a strong wind? Is it finding new fuel sources and growing quickly? Is the smoke turning from a fairly harmless white to gray to dark gray? The darker the smoke, the more intense the fire.

These lightning strikes happen all the time in the Southwest. It wasn't considered a big deal.

A crew of firemen from Mescalero had been flown in by helicopter to stop the blaze. They turned the job over to a bunch of hotshots from Sacramento, a crew of twenty, just like Granite Mountain. They partially contained the blaze and determined that it wasn't threatening any structures.

But the fire was stubborn, inventive, and it was burning in tough terrain where it was hard for the hotshots to maneuver. It kept growing. By the next day, it was a hundred-acre fire, having gotten a footing in the grasslands while still burning among the conifers. A grassland fire is the fastest fire out there. The hotshots built a fire line around the blaze, but it kept tossing off spot fires, blown by a wind that was now gusting to twenty miles per hour.

That afternoon, the fire began to "run." That is, it broke containment and started moving fast. It had turned into a thousand-acre fire. More hotshot crews were called in from Texas. It started to threaten housing tracts across a wide area, and people began to flee their homes. Mandatory evacuation was put into place.

The flame lengths had reached 150 feet. The fire was "out of control." That's a bit of a misnomer. The fire was in perfect control. It was controlling people's lives and the strategy of the hotshots.

The National Weather Service issued a red flag warning, and we got the call in Prescott that afternoon. We piled in the buggies and tore ass toward New Mexico. We were coming in toward Ruidoso on New Mexico State Road 48, a four-lane highway. We could see an advancing flank of the fire straight ahead of us, crimson-to-pink flames thirty and forty feet high. As we pulled up to a roadblock, we saw hundred-foot flames crowning over the highway. The flames were eating into a large two-story frame house on the right side of the road, just tearing that thing up. Behind the house was a big propane tank, which many homes in the rural parts of the Southwest use for heat. It was going up like a firework, spewing flames sixty feet in the air and getting ready to blow. It made this insane hissing noise as it got hotter.

Propane tanks are a bitch. They can wipe out a city block if one goes off. Dangerous as hell.

"No way we're getting through that," Eric said. "Let's find another way in."

We did a U-turn and swung back, looking for a road heading north that would take us to the fire. It took us two hours to get close. The fire kept moving and shutting down roads just before we got through. Finally, we reached a makeshift HQ and pulled in. Eric ran inside to get our assignment. Five minutes later, he came back out.

"Fire just burned up a housing complex. Complete loss. They're trying to reorganize, so they want us to hit town and grab lunch so we'll be ready later."

"Fuck," someone said. We were the cavalry and we were supposed to save the day, but the enemy was burning up everything in sight.

We couldn't do anything until we were assigned a sector; if you rush into a fire without a strategy, you're doing more harm than good. We went into Ruidoso, looking for a restaurant. We could see it was a mountain town a lot like Prescott, though somewhat smaller. People were running around with these worried looks on their faces, gathering up kids from school, running out to retirement homes to get grandparents. Some of their cars were loaded to the gills.

And here we were, the badass hotshots of Granite Mountain, stuffing our faces with roast beef sandwiches. As much of a bitch as it is to fight an out-of-control wildfire, we would have rather been risking our lives than sitting on our asses.

"Thank you," someone said as they passed our table.

We nodded, but inside we were like, *Please don't thank us until we've actually done something. This sucks.*

We were amped. Pissed off. Ready to go.

And we did. At Ruidoso, over the next six days, we kicked ass on the Little Bear Fire. We picked the right slopes to dig our firebreaks. We outworked it on its flanks and hemmed it in, one direction at a time. When it was threatening a development, our saws ripped through the chaparral and starved it of fuel. We worked flat out.

Ruidoso turned into the most destructive blaze in the history of New Mexico. It eventually took 242 homes, burned 44,000 acres, killed livelihoods, and cost a quarter of a billion dollars. It changed the lives of a lot of people.

But in our little sector of the blaze, we won. We saved the houses we were assigned to save, about a hundred of them, by my rough guess. And it felt incredible.

People came out on the fire line with home-cooked meals in their hands. The owners of motels in the area offered us free rooms if we wanted to rest and have a shower. (They were also offering the same to families who'd been burned out.) That wasn't new to us, but we were moved regardless. On some fires, we'd drive out and we'd see THANK YOU FIREFIGHTERS painted on the sides of barns in four-foot-high letters. It doesn't make the national news, but the local people will do anything for you.

Whenever you see a report about a wildfire on the news, you end up hearing the same line about what's been lost: "They're only things." You can replace a TV or a bed or a bunch of books; just go and buy new ones with the insurance money.

But I've come to believe that's bullshit. When you find

a woman who's snuck through the roadblocks to get to her burned-up house and she's inconsolable when she sees it, those aren't just "things" she's crying over. When you find a grandfather and he doesn't want the stereo or the strongbox with his life insurance in it, he just wants to find the American flag that the military gave him at his son's funeral— that's not what I call "things." It's their memories.

After Ruidoso, we drove back toward Prescott. We'd arrived on a fire that was ripping and now it was nothing at all. We were feeling good in that buggy, hooting and hollering about what we were going to do when we got home.

We passed by some roads where the fire had won. I saw people picking through the charred-out remains of their houses.

"Hey, guys," I called out. "I don't wanna kill your vibe, but especially the guys who are new, take a look around. These houses are burned to the ground. Stay on top of yourself out here, because that could be you. That could be your mom. This is why we train so hard. To make sure this shit doesn't happen."

Now that I think of it, maybe I'm more sensitive than most to the idea of home. Growing up practically a nomad with my mom, I was always searching for a place to call my own, where I could be with my family. A place that no one could take away from me.

The scary thing on the way back was driving through all those mountain towns strung along the highways of the Southwest and knowing any one of them could go up like Ruidoso, at any time. The hills were dry as dust. The drought was everywhere.

CHAPTER NINETEEN

In the summer of 2012, I was happy. It was my second season on the job I loved. I wanted to be in the woods for as long as I could.

I had made friends on the crew. The first was Chris MacKenzie. The dude who'd bullied me and enraged me. Chris and I, it turned out, had several things in common. We were both extremists, first of all. If we were going to do something, we were going to do it all the way.

Chris was the son of a firefighter and he'd grown up overweight. Grossly overweight. Throughout high school and after, he'd wheeze when he had to climb a set of stairs. But then, like me, he realized he wanted to be a hotshot, to follow in his father's footsteps.

That was that. He changed his diet completely, hit the gym, and within three months he lost seventy-five pounds. That was one reason he'd been so hard on me during training. For Chris, being a hotshot had changed his life. He wasn't going to accommodate some bozo off the street who didn't respect the job.

He even became my roommate. He'd been living in

Anthem, an hour away from Prescott, so he needed a place closer to the station. Natalie and I were living together at the time and she said there was no way he was moving in with us. I was caught in a bind: buddy versus girlfriend. Things weren't going well between Natalie and me. I saw that something in our relationship was contributing to the negatives in her life, that I was basically enabling Natalie by living with her. So I asked her to move back in with her parents. She did, and that was the end of me and Natalie. We were going down different paths, and separation was the best thing for both of us.

Chris and I started hanging out, and within a few weeks we were inseparable. We played video games together; ate breakfast, lunch, and dinner together; and worked together. When Easter or Thanksgiving rolled around, Chris would be over at my mom's house scarfing down her food.

He moved in and became like a second father to Michaela. We were two bros raising a little girl, and there was no doubt who was in charge: Michaela. One time, I was downstairs doing my laundry, with Chris upstairs watching my daughter. He needed to start washing some dishes, so he gave Michaela a big bag of veggie sticks to work on. He got to the sink and started soaping up the dishes when he heard Michaela calling him. Chris turned around. Michaela was holding the bag of veggie sticks. She locked eyes with my brother. Then she slowly turned the bag upside down and dumped out the veggies on the seats of our leather couch.

When I got back upstairs, Chris was laughing uncontrollably. "Dude, she never once took her eyes off of me."

She's a McDonough, I thought.

I found that, instead of aggressive and angry, Chris was

actually a very humble guy. A giving person. And calm. I can't even count the number of times I was getting ready to blow up at someone, and Chris would grab me by the shoulders and say, "Chill, Brendan. It's not that serious."

One time, after a blowout argument with Natalie, I came back to the apartment. I was so angry I could barely speak.

Chris watched me for a while, saying nothing, before he finally spoke up. "Dude, ask yourself one question."

"What?!" I yelled. "What one question?!"

"Where is this anger gonna get you?"

I told him to go to hell and stomped around some more. I may have thrown an object or two at the wall. But that thought stuck in my brain, and after a few more minutes I sat down on the couch.

"Guess you're right," I said.

Chris looked at me and thumbed down the volume on the TV. "You're going in the right direction. But that doesn't mean she's going to wake up and do the same. Doesn't work that way, and there's nothing you can do about it, bro."

I learned. I got better with Natalie. I was trying to be a new man.

One of the strange things about going straight was how it changed my friendships. Drug buddies are easy to talk to. You're stoned. Ninety percent of your conversation is a variant on the question "Where can we score?" Even the dumb stuff you say is funny.

But now that I was off drugs, I had to relate to people sober. I had to have actual conversations. Look people in the eye and learn how to listen. Plus, I had to find new things to talk about (my job, my family, sports). I felt like

I was the new kid in school all over again, but really I was just learning how to be a human being.

I quit drugs, but not drinking. Granite Mountain was a bunch of twenty- and thirty-something guys, and though some of them had sworn off alcohol, most of us hadn't.

One time during our offseason, Chris was going out drinking. I was taking a course at the fire academy and I was kicking ass. An ex-marine and I were neck and neck in all the physical stuff. I was finally in peak condition. I wanted to keep it that way.

"I'm going to hang out at home tonight," I told Chris.

"I'm sorry," he said, cocking his head. "Are you a bitch now?"

Stupid, juvenile stuff. But I couldn't help it. Chris knew how to get at me.

"Bitch? Chris, what did I tell you about that?"

"My bad."

I could have busted him in the face. I should have left well enough alone, but I couldn't let anyone say Brendan McDonough was not up to snuff.

"All right, man," I said, standing up and grabbing my keys. "Let's go."

I knew myself pretty well by that point. I had the presence of mind to call another friend. I told him that I was headed downtown to drink and it looked like it was going to be serious, so could he come to my apartment the next morning and take me to the fire academy? "Sure," he said. I left the door to my apartment unlocked so he could get in.

Then Chris and I went down to the bar and started drinking with a vengeance.

The next morning I woke up. My head felt like it was packed with wool and I could barely make it to the shower,

I was so exhausted. My buddy rolled in and found me sitting on my bed.

"Come on, Brendan, it's eight o'clock."

I didn't remember a damn thing from the night before. I got my clothes on and looked outside. My whole body was throbbing with a grade-A hangover.

Damn Chris MacKenzie to hell, I thought.

Chris and I grew close. We thought of each other as brothers. If he was out getting a sandwich for dinner, he automatically got me one. If I needed something, I turned to him first. And vice versa.

Once, when we were out on a fire, Chris got word that his mom had an accident at her home in California. She fell down some stairs and hit her head. When they gave her an MRI, they found a tumor inside her brain. They told her they'd have to operate in a couple of days.

Chris was devastated. But he didn't have the money for a plane ticket or even enough gas money to drive to Cali. He thought he'd wait until after the surgery, collect some funds, and go see her then.

Clayton heard what had happened. He found Chris and he put his arm around his shoulder.

"Dude, you need to go see your mom. You need to be with her."

Chris started explaining his predicament.

Clayton shook his head. "No, bro, you need to go. Now. I don't mean to scare you, but my mom had the same thing, and she ended up dying from it. I know what this thing can do. If you leave too late, you'll never forgive yourself."

We hadn't gotten paid for a couple of weeks. I had nothing to lend him. When you're making $12.83 an hour, you tend to live paycheck to paycheck.

"Do you think your mom would lend it to me?" Chris asked me. "I'm good for it, tell her..."

"Shut up, dude, I know you're good for it. Hell yes, I'll call her right now."

I called my mom. "Of course, I'll give him the money," she said. Chris drove three hours back to Prescott and she handed over the cash. He was so damn happy.

"Damn, dude," Chris said before he left. "Tell your mom I'll get it back to her on the twelfth, when I get paid."

"Don't even worry about it," I said.

He would have done the same for me. You can't put a price on a friendship like that.

Chris drove out that day to see his mom and be with her for the surgery. The doctors ended up removing the tumor. She made it through the surgery and made a complete recovery, and I was so thankful for that.

I'm not saying that Chris was an angel. He liked to mess with me. One time we were staging to fight a blaze in Carlsbad, New Mexico. "Staging" means they bring you in and tell you to get ready to hit the fire line, but they haven't assigned you a sector yet. So you're sitting around, waiting to go in. This particular morning, we went to an IHOP to load up on some breakfast before going into the field.

We were sitting at the table and Chris said, "Hey, Brendan. You look like you could be a waiter here."

I looked at him. "What the hell are you talking about?"

"You just look like a waiter. Take some orders, son!"

I stared him dead in the eye.

"You think I won't do that?"

He laughed. "That's exactly what I think."

I got up. The guys were smiling and nudging each other with their elbows. They probably thought I was just going to grab a paper and pencil and go to the other Granite Mountain table and goof off.

Hell no. I went back to the service area, where the waiters pick up the food. I nodded to a cook, who eyed me curiously over the steaming plates of pancakes and eggs, then found a bunch of aprons hanging off hooks. I grabbed one, took my time pulling it over my neck, then brought the straps around and tied them up front. Then I found a pad of paper and a pen and walked back out.

I didn't go to a Granite Mountain table. Too predictable. Instead, I spotted an elderly couple who'd just been seated and were studying menus.

"Good morning!" I said. "My name is Brendan and I'll be your server today. Can I get you started with some, uh, some juice or something?"

The woman looked me up and down.

"I've never seen you before. When did you start here?"

I could hear the guys behind me cracking up.

I told her this was my second day, and I took their order. Then I went to our table and played it cool, asking the guys what they wanted. Eric was shaking his head.

When I was done, I handed over my notes to the waitress. She was a cute dirty-blond-haired girl with great legs. When she asked who we were, someone told her we were firefighters. Before we left, the waitress wrote her number on a piece of paper and dropped it on our table. When we went back to IHOP the next morning, I left her the number for Chris's room. Returning the favor and all.

CHAPTER TWENTY

We were flying everywhere: Colorado, New Mexico, Idaho, Minnesota. The West was so dry that Granite Mountain barely had time to rest between jobs.

Early that season, after another two-week "roll" (or mission), I came home exhausted. I was lying on the couch in my apartment when Natalie called me.

"Brendan, we have a problem."

I sat up straight.

"What's wrong? Is Michaela all right?"

"She's fine." Natalie's voice sounded tense. "I mean, she's not fine. That's the point. She doesn't want to eat."

I was dumbfounded. I'd never heard of a child who didn't want to eat.

"What?"

"She misses you. She thinks that when you go away, you're never coming back. We have to deal with this."

I knew Michaela hated to see me go. Having a hotshot dad or mom is tough for a kid. You never know when your parent is going to disappear. We might be in the station and get the call to go to New Mexico or Idaho or Montana, and we'd get in the buggies and scoot. A quick call home, tears on the phone, and then we'd be out of touch for two weeks. Couldn't even call home. There's no cell phone signal in the middle of a national forest.

I tried to take it all in.

"She's not eating?"

"I took her to the doctor. He says she's suffering from separation anxiety and might be depressed."

That word was a sharp dagger. Depression. My mom had experienced it and so had I. But one-year-old girls shouldn't get depressed. It brought me back to that time I was twelve years old, crying my heart out in the driveway of my grandfather's house after my mom had gone to Oregon. At every stage, I seemed to see my life being repeated over in Michaela's. And each time, I had to fight to stop it from happening, to find a new way out for her.

I began to realize that eventually I'd have to take a job fighting structure fires, so that I could have regular hours and see my daughter more often. I was also going through a custody fight for Michaela, and I knew that if I didn't have a nine-to-five, I'd barely see her.

Later on, I talked to Jesse and he took me in to see Eric. I repeated the story to Eric and told him that I needed to look at the structure side. At one point, I was explaining that Michaela had stopped eating when I left. I started crying.

Second time I'd cried in front of the man. Damn. But the thought that I was causing my daughter such pain was hard to take.

Eric didn't want to lose guys. If he liked you, he wanted to keep you on Granite Mountain. I was worried about that.

But he surprised me. "Listen, Brendan," he said. "Whatever you need to do for your daughter, you go ahead and do that. I support you fully. You got that?"

I nodded, unable to speak. I'd never had that from a man—that unconditional support, that love. It meant a lot to me.

The three of us talked about when I would start moving over to the structure side. Eric made it clear that it was up to me: When I was ready, he'd make some calls and try to get me started with Prescott Fire. Meanwhile, I was still a part of his hotshots.

Until that moment, maybe I didn't really believe that Granite Mountain was 100 percent real. I'd met many people in my life who talked about having your back when it counted, but few of them had come through for me. The drug business is not the best place to learn about loyalty.

Eric needed bodies for the line, but he needed me to be a good father more. I cried because I knew all those words Eric had used—"integrity," "love"—weren't just words to him. He meant to stand by them. To live them out.

Granite Mountain had become my substitute family.

CHAPTER TWENTY-ONE

The Doce Fire kicked off on June 18, 2013. It ran fast and hot. It was unstoppable, eventually burning upward of eleven square miles of terrain. Some guys made a joke that it was eating the brush like Hungry Hungry Hippos. And it was threatening Prescott. Our home.

This was the fire where Chris and I nearly got caught by the fire wall; we tossed our drip torches into the flames and barely made it out alive.

We fought the fire for three days, and most of that time, it straight-up kicked our asses. It would slop over our containment lines, jump our breaks. On the third day, as we were heading back from the fire line, the situation went from depressing to ridiculous, or so I thought. "We've been asked to save a juniper tree," Jesse told us.

We were tired, our eyes red from constant smoke.

"A juniper tree?" I asked. "What the fuck for? There's *billions* of 'em out there."

"Not like this one," Jesse said. "It's the world's largest alligator juniper and it's right in our backyard. It's like a national treasure, okay? Tomorrow we're going to go in there and assess and see if we can save it."

That piqued my interest. I jumped on the Internet and started looking up this bad boy. I found one story about this guy who made a pilgrimage and came to Prescott to find this amazing tree. He asked around, but there were no maps or coordinates to tell the visitor where to look. Finally, he stumbled on a local who knew where it was and agreed to take him there. Together, they hiked out to the spot and found the tree and took pictures. The man was overjoyed.

The next day, we parked the buggies and hiked in. The tree was about a mile and a half from the trailhead. When we found it, it was big and beautiful: a thick-trunked old boy with low, spreading branches. I wondered how many of the junipers in this area it had spawned. It was like being in the Garden of Eden, Southwest style, with the original juniper.

We got our saws out and began cutting brush and digging line around the tree until we had a nice containment zone. Now we needed to burn it out so that any wildfire approaching the place wouldn't be able to burn through. Andrew and Dustin Deford got the job, and we could see the smoke rising as they lit the fire. We worked all day until darkness had fallen, then jumped in the buggies and headed to a Red Robin for dinner.

We were all chowing down on our hamburgers when a guy from Prescott Fire walked over. He asked us what we'd been working that day and we looked at each other a little sheepishly. "Actually, we were saving the world's oldest alligator juniper," Jesse said.

"Are you serious?" the guy answered. "I asked my wife to marry me under that thing!"

This juniper was sacred to people. We'd spent our

careers destroying juniper—it was like the number one fuel in the Southwest.

We followed the reports trickling in from the field that night. We knew the fire was blitzing the hills near the oldest tree, and we were downhearted. Not too much was going to survive a wildfire on parched high desert. The next morning, we woke up worried about the damn thing. *Is the tree okay? Did it make it through the night?* We felt a sense of ownership now. As the rest of the crew headed off to work, Jesse hiked in to the tree to see if the thing was still standing.

"Granite Mountain," we heard Jesse on the radio at about ten a.m.

"Go ahead."

"She's standing, all right. Just one big branch burning from an ember. But I dug it out and everything's cool now."

After that, the juniper became like a talisman for us. The next day my squad hiked out there to eat lunch next to it. It threw a lot of shade and we sat under it and ate our packed lunches.

Don't ask me how, but we got on the subject of Job, from the Bible. Maybe the antiquity of the tree, everything it had seen, got us thinking on deeper things. Maybe someone in the crew was talking about how nothing was going right for them, how they felt like Job, facing one calamity after another.

There were a bunch of Christians on that squad. I was a believer, someone who tried to follow Jesus as best I could. Clayton, Dustin, and Wade Parker were all men of faith. So the discussion went around and around about Job and what he meant.

"What would you do if you lost everything?" I said to Wade.

"I'd trust in God," he said.

"If you lost your family, all of them? I mean everything, Wade."

"So do I."

I looked at Wade to see if he was fucking with me. But his face was calm. He gave his answers without a moment's hesitation.

I was so struck by that. Wade and the boys were ready for any disaster, for any loss, no matter how painful. Because they had something bigger behind them—their love for God. That idea of giving up everything to the Lord, and doing it easily, with a glad heart, that just floored me. I vowed that day to be a better Christian. To be more like Clayton and Dustin and Wade. I wanted the serenity they had.

Our half-hour lunch turned into an hour before we had to pack up and walk out.

"Man, that was the most I've heard about God in my entire life," Grant McKee said as we marched single-file along the trail.

I was fired up. "If you want, I'll go to church with you," I said. I felt closer to Jesus than I had since I was a child.

Saving that ancient tree, that part of God's creation, had brought me closer to Christ, and I wanted to share it with my brothers. Grant and I made plans to go to Mass together in a few weeks when we both had time.

It still bothers me that we never made it.

CHAPTER TWENTY-TWO

Central Arizona lies in what is known as the Transition Zone, mountainous terrain that is bordered by the dry Colorado Plateau to the north and the wetter Basin and Range Province to the south. It borrows characteristics from both of those landscapes: steep terrain and spur ridges alternating with flat valleys. The dominant plant types are juniper, turbinella oak, catclaw acacia, and manzanita. The combination of high ridges and level valleys makes the weather across the terrain highly local and variable. Conditions can change quickly in a relatively small area.

Every summer, usually in late June, a change occurs in the weather over central Arizona. Wet, colder air moves up from Mexico and pushes out the warmer, drier air that's lain over the land all spring. In that meeting of cold and warm air, thunderstorms form, and as they get bigger they draw in the heat that's been building up over the early summer. Then they go roaming over the high desert, dropping rain. In terms of wind, thunderstorms produce a range of effects: microbursts, gust fronts, outflows.

Every part of the country gets thunderstorms, but in the Southwest, they have a special significance: They can turn a gentle, meandering blaze into a blowtorch.

A storm during monsoon season is a double-edged sword, either helpful or hurtful depending on one factor: moisture. A wet thunderstorm can bring pounding rains, which can cool off fires or even put them out completely. But a dry thunderstorm pushes strong, unstable winds that can make a fire much hotter and faster moving. Some dry thunderstorms actually produce rain, but the air in the Southwest is so parched that the rain evaporates even before it hits the ground.

On June 28, 2013, an early-summer thunderstorm formed near a town called Yarnell, about thirty miles southwest of Prescott. This was the first big thunderstorm of the season, and the wet Mexican winds hadn't fully occupied the terrain. There was little moisture for the winds to pick up. And much of the moisture the thunderstorm was carrying was in the form of ice crystals.

In the jostling streams of hot and cold air, the crystals collided. Electrons were sheared away from the ice molecules. They formed an intense electrical field, with thousands of volts per inch. Current began to flow. In the process, the surface of the earth became positively charged. When a filament of negatively charged particles intersects with a high point on the earth's surface, the air heats to fifty thousand degrees Fahrenheit, five times hotter than the sun. Lightning flashes down to the dry terrain.

In the towns of central Arizona, things were tinder dry that summer. In Yarnell, the last good rain had been on March 7, and there'd been a light shower in early April that dropped a tenth of an inch of rain on the town and the surrounding hills, which was quickly sucked up by the oak roots and the cacti. The National Climatic Data Center, which monitors weather associated with drought, reported that there was "an abnormally dry fuel bed" in the area around the town that spring. A state agency, the Southwest Coordination Center—which has a Predictive Services section that attempts to pinpoint wildfire conditions in different localities—issued an advisory for the Yarnell area. Tucked into the bulletin was a section called "Concerns to Firefighters and the Public." It listed four predictions for the coming fire season:

1. Surface fire will quickly transition to crown fire and only requires low to moderate surface fire intensity to transition.
2. Active/running crown fire has produced long-range spotting up to one mile under the influence of an unstable atmosphere.
3. Active fire behavior can extend well into night and early morning hours even with moderate relative humidity recovery.
4. Thunderstorm activity will create a mosaic pattern of surface fuel moistures[;] surface fire intensity and fire behavior may change abruptly when fires cross these boundaries of moist and dry surface fuels.

The predictions would all prove accurate. Points one and four would become especially important.

The conditions foreseen by the coordination center were confirmed on the ground. By May 17, a captain with the Yarnell Fire Department reported that the "danger of wildfire in the Yarnell area reached the maximum level

(Extreme)...The scrub oaks, pine trees, untamed shrubs and dry grasses are all perfect fuels for a wildfire."

There was no rain at all in May or June. In late June, the calculated probability of ignition for Yarnell and the surrounding area was measured at 60 percent for shaded areas (of which there were few) and 90 percent for unshaded areas.

Residents of the town had watched the huge mushroom smoke cloud from the Doce Fire in Prescott in mid-June and wondered if their decades-long run of good luck was over. Smoke on the horizon means something different than it did in frontier days. Then it meant a possible Indian raid. Now it means wildfire.

The thunderstorms arrived over Yarnell on June 28. On a ridge west of Yarnell, a flash of lightning hit a patch of rocky terrain at 5:36 p.m. The point of contact was probably a tall stand of manzanita or a juniper bush. The strike ignited the scrub oak, and flames sprouted across the ridge. But winds were mild and the fire only managed to sputter across half an acre that day.

When local residents called in reports of smoke, an Air Attack plane was sent out to spot the fire. After being unable to find it, the pilot finally radioed back that the flames were located in a boulder field on a west-facing slope, inaccessible to vehicles, and they were barely smoking.

It was a typical Arizona high desert wildfire. Hilly terrain at between 4,500 and 6,000 feet. Juniper, scrub oak, some pine. Very dry conditions. Public land, managed by the Arizona Department of Forestry, which provides for the prevention and suppression of wildland fire on 22 million acres of Arizona State Trust Land and private property.

Our bread and butter, you might say. That day, June 28, there were thirty-seven active fires in Arizona, and Yarnell was one of the smaller ones. The land across the state was bone dry, aching to burn.

For the first day, Yarnell was a nothing fire. Spread potential was marked down as "minimal." But on the second day, June 29, the fire began to grow, pushed by stronger winds. Two single-engine air tankers (or SEATs) arrived over the scene midmorning and dropped four loads of fire retardant on the blaze.

Just before eleven a.m., a helicopter from the BLM ferried in the first contingent of firefighters to battle the blaze. Six of the men were from the Arizona Department of Corrections—prison firefighters—and one was a "helitack" (short for helicopter attack firefighter). The men were dropped about a quarter mile from the ridge and began cutting fire line to contain the blaze.

The retardant penned the flames in on the western and southern flanks. A stone ridge was holding the fire in on the north and an old two-track road formed a natural barrier on the east. By that afternoon, the fire had grown to two acres, but it was still contained in its natural and manmade box. That afternoon, fire officials kept the two SEAT aircraft on hold until the Incident Commander voluntarily released one of them to go fight another fire.

The typical afternoon breezes that bring relief to Arizonans arrived and the fire grew again. Officials now requested the return of the previously released SEAT, along with an Air Attack plane to do recon and direct other firefighting aircraft. The SEAT returned several hours later.

The weather forecast for that day was grim. The temperature was expected to reach 105 degrees and the relative humidity was headed toward a dry, but not atypical, 11 percent. Perhaps most ominously, the National Weather Service issued a report about a storm cell developing to the northeast of Yarnell. A thunderstorm that might push toward Yarnell was developing. Storms mean wind, and wind is often the great variable in just how dynamic a fire can get.

Winds from the west-southwest continued to stoke the flames higher. The fire jumped the two-track road and began rolling east. The blaze had now broken containment and was ranging through terrain officials had originally thought beyond its reach. Six more firefighters were eventually flown in to help with the "slop-over." They dug a fire line as the flames roared in their ears. They knew that most of the buildings and people threatened by the fire lay to their east, so they worked furiously to stop the fire moving in that direction. By five thirty p.m., one of the Department of Corrections crews had run out of chainsaw gas, which cut their effectiveness drastically.

The fire was getting bigger and hotter. Its "operational complexity and tempo continue[d] to escalate," according to a report from the Yarnell Hill Fire Serious Accident Investigation. Fire officials requested a large air tanker (LAT) and a Type 1 heavy helitanker, both of which carry more retardant than the single-engine aircraft. But at 5:42 p.m., the requested LAT and the helitanker canceled their runs; winds were too high along their flight paths. There was another option: a VLAT, or very large air tanker, a turbofan DC-10 that's been converted to a tanker. These enormous planes can carry 11,400 gallons of rust-red retardant in belly-mounted tanks and release their entire load in eight seconds.

There are only two active VLATs in the entire country. Luckily, one of them was stationed in Albuquerque—just 450 miles from Yarnell—and the weather was good for takeoff. But there were other things to consider: The

VLAT is expensive, costing around $57,000 for every load of retardant, which means it's usually reserved for large fires. Yarnell, though uncontained, was still categorized as a small blaze. There was also a concern that terrain around Yarnell was too steep for the VLAT to be effective. With darkness approaching (tankers don't fly after nightfall), the decision was made not to bring in the VLAT. The stated reason was "fire conditions."

Late in the afternoon, the fire continued to outrun its boundaries. The small SEATs were still dropping retardant, but the scale of the fire had grown beyond their capabilities. The temperature at 5:24 p.m. was 101 degrees, with relative humidity at 12 percent and sustained winds of 10 mph, gusting to 20. The fire was eating through the chaparral at 100 to 200 yards per hour, with flame lengths between 10 and 20 feet.

The incident commander working Yarnell knew that if they didn't stop the fire by nightfall, it could make a run in the morning and be in position to burn houses, even entire towns. The flames were now a mile from a small town called Peeples Valley and less than 1.5 miles from Yarnell. There were people there, horses, double-wide trailers, shops, government offices, homes. These weren't the mansions in the hills that hotshots are often sent out to protect. They were the homes of working-class people, retirees, ex-servicemen on modest incomes, people who'd drifted out to the desert and found it to their liking. Ordinary Americans.

At 5:48 p.m., the Incident Commander in charge of the fire reported that it represented a threat to Yarnell and Peeples Valley in the approaching 24 to 48 hours.

Dusk came on. The horizon was lit by layers of purple and luminescent gray. There was mixed news that evening. The storm cell that the National Weather Service had spotted was fading; its winds wouldn't threaten Yarnell. That was a relief to anyone who knows how wildfires behave.

But the fire continued its pattern of exceeding the expectations of the men and women attempting to control it. At 7:38 p.m., it had spread to one hundred acres, which meant that in twelve hours, it had grown fifty times larger. It was stubborn. It was seeking a breakout.

All night, fire officials called in bulldozers, fire engines, structure crews, and aircraft for the morning attack. The residents of Yarnell watched the flames glowing in the darkness that night. They had to level their eyes up slightly to see them. The hills blended with the darkness of the skies so that it appeared that the fire was floating above their heads. The flames were an enormous red-orange scar in the night sky.

Many residents had never seen a fire this big this close to their homes. Their hope was that the flames would "lay down"—that is, subside—during the night. They prayed for the winds to lessen. The 911 line was busy with calls.

By 10:00 p.m., a fire official called the Yavapai County Sheriff's Office and told him to be ready to give local residents the evacuation orders. These are known as "reverse 911 calls." There are no sirens or other means of emergency notification in Yarnell. If residents didn't hear the phone or get the email, they wouldn't know when the evacuation had begun.

Just before midnight, a supervisor jumped in his truck and went scouting along the back roads of Yarnell, surveying the town's defenses. What he found were yards filled with trees right up to the siding, lots overgrown with shrubs and pine, roofs overhung with branches of dry pine. There hadn't been a big fire in the area since 1966. Perhaps people had gotten to thinking one was never coming. Many of the houses the supervisor drove by were, from a firefighting point of view, completely indefensible.

If the fire reached Yarnell, the supervisor concluded, Yarnell would burn.

Some residents stayed up all night watching the progress of the flaming front. But others thought they might get lucky one more time. As one resident later wrote, these people "went to bed that night, assuming they were safe, as always."

CHAPTER TWENTY-THREE

The day before Granite Mountain headed to Yarnell, June 29th, I'd gone to a funeral. It was for the father of a friend of mine who I'd gotten close to during my partying days. I would crash at my friend's house when I needed a place to sleep, and his parents—both of them strong Christians—welcomed me every single time. They always accepted and loved me for who I was and not what I happened to be doing at the time, and I'd always appreciated them for that. A week before the Yarnell fire, the father had passed away and I'd asked Jesse if I could attend the funeral. He said if the crew wasn't working a fire, he'd do his best to let me off; I was also sick with the flu, so he told me to get checked out by a doctor. Jesse had been as good as his word, and the funeral had turned into a true celebration of the man's life and his deep concern for other people. I was so touched by how many people turned out to pay tribute to this good man.

That night, Chris, Garret Zuppiger, and I had dinner at one of our favorite restaurants, the Park Plaza Liquor & Deli. We'd had a few beers, munched on some pizza, then hit a bar on the way home for a nightcap. An average night that led to an average morning.

June 30 was my first day back. I returned filled with that feeling I'd experienced at the funeral—of how worthwhile life can be if you live it with compassion. I felt good about things.

When we got to the station, Eric was in his office. I heard him on the phone figuring out the plan for the day. The original idea was that we'd be heading to Prescott National Forest, where a wildfire had been burning for days; we'd be pre-positioned there for any flare-ups. But after a few minutes, Eric came out and told us we were assigned to Yarnell. He gave us a quick briefing and we geared up for the ride south.

It had been a tough month for the crew. We'd been working fires for twenty-eight out of the thirty days of June, and the rest of the guys had been going twelve days straight, without a break. It was an unusually active stretch for us.

I knew Yarnell. As a teenager, I'd become buddies with a kid whose family had a ranch nearby. I'd spent countless hours there, horsing around with him and our friends or target shooting in the local hills. It was a small mountain town like Prescott, just not so big or populated. When evening fell, you could feel the shape of the enormous granite boulders that crown the local ridges. Black against a blue-black starred sky.

Yarnell had been founded by a small band of gold prospectors in the 1860s. It's a typical story from the Old West. But these prospectors—including one man, an explorer named Pauline Weaver—actually found nuggets lying on the exposed rock, which wasn't typical at all. *Hot damn*, they must have thought, *this is the place*. They named the outcropping Rich Hill and the town became Yarnell, and it had years of plenty and it had bad times, too. During the Great Depression, the town's population dipped to just eighteen people. Yarnell tended to attract hardy, independent-minded types, "desert refugees," they were sometimes called. Its high altitude and cool summer temperatures made it into a retreat for people escaping Phoenix summers. "The most perfect place within the civilized world," one of its residents described it to a newspaper reporter in the 1950s.

The town was founded on gold, but it survived because of the relief it offered from the hot gusts of the Sonoran Desert, which lies 1,700 feet below. Even the town's motto centers on wind: "Where the desert breeze meets the mountain air." In 2013, its population hovered around 650.

Geographically, Yarnell is slotted in between two ridges of the Weaver Mountains, with one main road—State Route 89—running through it. It's a place most people blow past on their way to Prescott or Phoenix and forget about before the last storefront has flashed by. It's too small to have a town council, a police department, or even a mayor—but they damn well have a fire department. You have to in central Arizona. For everything else, if something needs doing, a guy or a girl gets off their ass and does it. Simple as that.

There are old mining towns like Yarnell strung all along the highways of Arizona and New Mexico. The people there like the mountains, like the freedom, and don't miss Boston or Chicago one bit. They sit outside their houses in the afternoon and wait for the cool breeze that often comes after lunch. Talk about the chances of rain. Live their lives.

It was like a lot of places hotshots end up in the summer months. Places most people have never heard of.

I was a bit sleepy and as soon as I got in the buggy that

morning, I closed my eyes and got some sleep. The hum of the tires on the road put us to sleep. Sometimes you can be on a fire for thirty-six hours straight, so you take any opportunity to rest up for it.

When we stopped at the Yarnell Fire Station at around eight a.m. on June 30, I stretched and stepped out into the bright sunlight. It was hot as a rattlesnake's belly. *Damn*, I thought, *we're gonna sweat out there*.

I scanned the horizon until I spotted smoke. There it was, on a ridge about a mile away, light gray, barely puffing. The fire was just skunking around, not doing much of anything.

"Hell, dude, this thing looks assed out!" I called to Chris, who was yawning. "We're going to be home in time for supper tomorrow."

Chris laughed. "Hope so," he said.

As ominous as the fire was to the people of Yarnell, we'd seen far worse.

Most of the guys headed off to get a briefing, to find out what the fire was doing, hash out tactics, check weather reports, and decide which radio frequency everyone was going to be on. The fire chiefs were studying a map of Yarnell and the surrounding area on an iPad loaded with Google Maps. They knew what assets were available: their own fire department with their volunteers, fourteen Type 6 fire engines, six water tenders, two bulldozers, three Type 1 hotshot crews (for attacking the fire, although one crew was ultimately unable to respond due to vehicle mechanical trouble), two Type 2 crews (for containment and mop-up), with additional crews made up of inmates from two Arizona prisons, Yuma and Lewis. From the air, officials put in the call for three airborne tankers, four SEATs, six heli-tankers, and the DC-10 out of Albuquerque.

The guys returned and we got in our trucks. A fellow named Gary Cordes, who was in charge of structure protection, drove with us, showing us the terrain. One place he pointed out on the map was Boulder Springs Ranch. It's owned by a semi-retired couple and filled with western art: huge strands of barbed wire as thick as a man's waist, along with other curiosities. The owners had cleared the land of trees and shrubs and their structures were made of fire-resistant materials. It was an ideal safety zone, safe as anything in the area. "Bombproof," Cordes called it. "Of course, you also have the black," he added.

The supervisors that morning set a series of trigger points. If the fire reached a ridge one mile north of Yarnell, residents would be ordered to evacuate. A second trigger was established closer to the town—if that one was breached, firefighters themselves would be ordered to leave. The third trigger, a ridge right on the edge of Yarnell, was the last-ditch point: If the fire hit it, anyone remaining in the town was to retreat immediately.

In Boise, Idaho, 860 miles away, officials at the National Interagency Coordination Center were watching the fire. The NICC is a clearinghouse for wildland firefighters. Every blaze in the country is monitored and assessed and firefighting assets are parceled out according to availability and need. That morning, Yarnell was in the middle of the pack. It was rated as a Type 2 fire, one of several that were active in the early-morning hours.

The fire had grown again and was now roaming between three hundred and five hundred acres. People in Yarnell began making their way to the higher ground east of the town to try to get an eye on the flames. On the way, they saw firefighters and hotshots arriving.

At the briefing, the fire chiefs decided to set an anchor point at the southwest heel of the fire, to keep it from running at Yarnell. Granite Mountain got the job.

Our buggies began threading their way past mobile homes and small houses along Yarnell's Sesame Street, everything cooking in the heat. The asphalt ran out and we were on dirt roads now, branches scraping the sides of the buggies with a nails-on-a-chalkboard sound. We parked the buggies on the side of Sesame and got out as Eric drove ahead in his supervisor's truck to scout some more. We trudged ahead on foot and found his truck farther up the slope, parked in a clearing to keep it away from any advancing fire.

We got ready to hike in to the fire line, checking our tools and saws. We guzzled as much water as we could and slung extra bottles of it onto our packs. The guys made their final calls to their families before leaving their phones in the trucks—many of them didn't carry their cells into a fire, as reception in the hills was often spotty or nonexistent.

Eric radioed back to Jesse, telling him he'd found a route in. We headed down the dirt road that led all the way to the top of the ridge, with Jesse in the lead. The hill was dusty, dried-out vegetation to our left and right, the only sounds the tramping of our feet and the occasional warble of a songbird. Tangles of chaparral. The shrubs around us had grown thick and twisted in the last fifty years. They were ten feet high in places, with pines studded here and there reaching to twenty feet.

The scrub was nothing abnormal, but it was thicker than in most places we worked. In your mind, as you walk, there's a little calculator adding up the amount and the type of fuel around you. Square footage times height times density. I knew there was a shit-ton of chaparral ready to go up if the fire came this way.

The fire was chewing steadily north, away from our position. It was now threatening the homes of a subdivision called Model Creek in Peeples Valley. At 10:45 a.m., the fire chiefs ordered the people from Model Creek and the nearby Double Bar A Ranch evacuated. Cars rolled down the dirt roads as residents brought their dogs and cats to the nearby Muleshoe Animal Clinic for safekeeping. Bigger animals, including horses, were loaded into trailers and released into pens at a place called Hidden Springs Ranch.

We were heading toward the southwest side of the fire, which was mostly burning to the north-northeast.

There were problems in the air above us. Only two of the requested four SEATs were flying and dropping retardant. The other two were out of commission with mechanical problems. They hoped to join the fight later in the day, but every hour was critical. And at 9:40 a.m., two of the heavy tankers had been called off Yarnell and headed to another wildfire, in Kingman.

There was just too much fire across Arizona to devote everything to ours.

I kept my eyes on the trail, looking for snakes, trying to pace myself. The air felt humid, though I knew that wasn't possible. The sun was drying out the air quick. We were at about five thousand feet, almost a mile above sea level.

When we got to the top of the ridge, we took a look at the fire. We were high enough up that we were looking level at the flames eating through the brush to the north. Eric gave us a quick briefing: The weather was super hot and windy. Homes were being threatened. It was our job to keep the flames from heading toward Yarnell and the nearby town of Glen Ilah. If things got hot, the escape route was through the black or to the "bombproof" safety zone, Boulder Springs Ranch.

"I need a short squad," Eric said. "We got any volunteers?"

I stepped up, along with Scott Norris, Billy, and Dustin. Eric chose me as the lead.

I smiled. That felt good. It was the first time he'd ever done that.

"We're gonna take these guys and button up the anchor, okay?"

"Sure thing," I said.

"Okay. I'll walk you to the heel."

The five of us headed to the back side of the mountain, walking along the two-track road we'd come in on. (This also happened to be an old firebreak, which was a plus.) Eric pointed out the spot he wanted us to carve out as the anchor point, which was a section of an old trail. He then headed north, scouting. He told us he'd call on the radio if he needed us to change position.

Billy and I got our Pulaski tools out and began scraping at the ground, clearing a two-foot barrier down to the bare mineral soil, tearing out brush and roots and leaving a clean firebreak, while Scott and Dustin cut and swamped with a chainsaw. The old trail separated the green from the black, so we were basically cleaning up the old trail while the saw team cut a few feet of brush on each side, looking for any sign of heat. (This is called cold-trailing.) I wanted to dig out a few cup trenches—ditches on the downhill slope of a hill that has the possibility of burning. You dig a nice little trench, form a lip or a berm on the downslope edge, and that baby will catch material rolling down the hill that might light up brush farther down the hill. We dug a few of those.

At 10:30 a.m., the fire's front was a 1.5-mile-long line of burning brush, still moving in a northerly direction. By 11:00, the fire had grown to 1,500 acres. Flame lengths were at fifteen to twenty feet. A DC-10 was droning overhead, dumping its loads of nearly twelve thousand gallons of retardant.

The wind was fitful, and the sun was riding high in a blue sky. Every so often I glanced at the smoke on the horizon. It was getting a little thicker and darkening. A fire is always either growing or dying out, and this one was growing.

Thirty minutes later, we'd almost cleared out the anchor point. No flames were going to get past here unless they were massive, arcing over to the chaparral on the other side. Sweat was pouring down my face as I saw Eric approaching in his red hard hat.

He pitched in and helped us clear the last half chain—that is, ten yards—of line.

"Looks good, Donut. Nice work."

I felt a surge of pride. Eric didn't give out praise that often. I knew the anchor was tight—I'd learned enough in the last two years to tell a sloppy job from a first-rate one.

It was a tiny moment of satisfaction. I felt like I knew what I was doing. I'd earned Eric Marsh's trust. That meant a great deal to me.

We headed back and found the main group. They were burning backfires on the upslope, lighting chaparral and letting it crackle, depriving the fire of any fuel if it doubled back to the south. A few of the guys were working their drip torches, and we watched as the flames licked up on the shrubs.

After the fire ate up about a chain of scrub oak, at 11:36 a.m., a plane flew overhead and dumped some retardant on the area, killing the burn. "Shit," Eric said, annoyed. "What the hell are they doing?" About ten minutes later, another tanker came swooping in and laid another coat of retardant, pissing Eric off again. The pilots were clearly trying to pretreat the green sections, but they were misjudging the distance.

At noon, an ASM, or aerial supervision module—a fixed-wing aircraft with two crew members aboard—arrived over Yarnell. Its job was to coordinate the airborne assets in attacking the fire, manage air traffic, work on tactics, and actually lead the drop planes to their target. The crew would be another set of eyes on the fire line.

Eric decided we would go direct—head straight to the burning edge of the fire and cut line there. He and Jesse were talking. I bent down to tie my shoelace and when I looked up, Jesse motioned me over.

"Hey, Donut, what do you think of taking lookout?"

"Sure," I said. I wasn't particularly excited about the job. Being a lookout meant standing in the sun and baking while staring at the same patch of land. But it's a key part of the work.

"You got your weather kit?"

I checked. "Yes, sir."

Working lookout is just what it sounds like. You find an ideal spot from which to observe the fire (which is often different from where the crew is cutting line) and you watch it and the weather. You are the eyes of the crew. You measure the temperature and the probability of ignition. You monitor incoming weather and cloud formations. Basically, you're a one-man early-warning system for any potential danger.

I looked around for a spot to perch. At first I thought I'd stay close to the crew, but as I surveyed the terrain I saw there wasn't a natural lookout spot anywhere within fifty yards. But out farther was an opening in the brush that would give me a wide-angle view of the landscape and the fire.

I pointed it out to Jesse and Eric. "How about there?" It was a rocky outcropping in a section of flat ground, about half a mile away to the northeast, closer to where the fire was whipping ahead.

They turned their heads and nodded. Done.

I heard the sound of a UTV, and sure enough one rolled up on us. On board were two hotshots, the superintendent and a captain, from the Blue Ridge crew. Blue Ridge was based in the Coconino National Forest, near Flagstaff, and they'd been called in that day just like Granite Mountain. The crew was working about half a mile downslope from us, at the base of the hill.

Time to do the weather. I took out my wet thermometer, dipped the wick, and started spinning it. As I got my readings, the Blue Ridge guys were asking about a lookout. "That's him," Jesse said, pointing to me. The super, Brian Frisby, asked me if I wanted a ride to the clearing. I said, "Hell yeah."

I relayed my weather readings to Jesse and Eric, then packed my stuff for the ride to the lookout point. "Catch you later," I said to Eric.

Eric smiled. "This side or the other, brother." I thought nothing of it. It was an everyday thing to say.

"Why do they call you Donut?" Brian asked. I explained as we walked toward the UTV.

The day's strategy was clear. Granite Mountain would stay on the anchor of the fire in the southwest, while most of the resources—air and ground—would be concentrated on the "head" of the fire in the north. The boys would cut chaparral and dig line along the edge of the fire. They'd chop out a piece of line, then see if it held before moving on. We'd have three sets of eyes on the fire: me, Eric, and Jesse near the crew. We'd be linked by radio to Blue Ridge and the rest of the personnel working Yarnell, as well as the spotters in the air.

I got on the UTV along with Brian and the Blue Ridge captain. Brian whipped it around and I got my last glimpse of the boys as they headed into the brush, their bodies leaning forward, their heads tilted down. The camera in my brain clicked and I looked over Brian's shoulder at the terrain ahead.

CHAPTER TWENTY-FOUR

The fire was defeating every effort to contain it. Supervisors wanted the second DC-10 assigned to Yarnell (it took off at 1:04 p.m. and headed toward the fire). They got on the phone and requested two more heavy tankers to drop water. The NICC in Boise, which was moving its planes and hotshot teams from fire to fire, gave them only one. It was the same story with helitankers: The call went out for two. Yarnell got half that.

The Blue Ridge guys and I made our way down the mountain. I was heading toward the rock outcropping I'd spotted from the staging area where Granite Mountain was now working. Once the road ran out, I got off.

"Call us on the radio if you need a lift out," Brian said as I headed in. I waved to him and began walking along a thin trail until I came to an old dozer that had apparently conked out. Another dozer had cleared a wide area around it, hoping to preserve it if the fire came this way. I was heading toward the fire. Nothing too worrying. The blaze was continuing its steady north-northeast push.

I passed a large wash—a space where water has cleared

out some of the vegetation—on my right. It was free of oak brush. *I don't think I'm going to have to deploy, but if I did, this would be the spot*, I said to myself. I was alone now; I had to make my own contingency plans. Deploying my fire shelter was the last resort, but it was good to find someplace to do it.

I walked a few chains past the dozer until I found the flat rock I'd spotted earlier, which was about 120 yards north of the clearing behind me. I looked at the fire, then got out my radio and my weather kit. This would be my headquarters until further notice.

The sun was really cooking now. I could feel the heat rising off the rock I was standing on. I did the weather and sure enough, the PIG—probability of ignition, which measures temperature, relative humidity, and elevation—was up. The air was getting drier and hotter. That meant conditions were more conducive to the spread of the fire, but this was to be expected on a hot afternoon. I gave my weather report on the radio and Eric and a bunch of other guys on the crew copied it.

I scanned the horizon. Most of the action was on the other side of the ridge. I let the boys know where they were. I looked down onto the terrain and found a spot that would be my trigger point, a drainage ditch about 300 yards from where I stood. If the fire backed its way to my trigger point, I would move out immediately and make my way back toward the cleared ground around the old dozer.

Lunchtime. I pulled an MRE out of my pack, ripped open the lid, dosed it with my bottle of Tabasco, and ate. I've always believed that Tabasco could make Kevlar edible, and the hiking had left me hungry. I wolfed down the meal as I listened to Jesse's voice come over the radio.

Granite Mountain was stopping for lunch, too. Once they'd finished, they'd stay where they were. They weren't planning on going direct to the fire any farther unless they got more support.

By 1:00 p.m., officials closed Route 89 heading south to Yarnell. It was now too dangerous for vehicles. A Forestry official worked up a complexity analysis on the fire and recommended that the response be upgraded to a Type 1 Incident Management Team, or IMT, meaning that specially trained and experienced firefighters be called in to fight it. The recommendation went up the chain of command, but the district forester on the fire and the fire marshal agreed that the blaze was even more serious. They wanted a Type 1 IMT, the highest designation. The request was relayed to Boise.

At 2:02 p.m., the Flagstaff office of the National Weather Service updated the weather picture. A thunderstorm on the fire's east side was predicted to produce outflow winds of thirty-five to forty-five miles per hour. The winds were going to change and reverse direction. Bad news for Granite Mountain. A forty-five-mile-per-hour wind can alter a fire completely. The danger goes up by an order of magnitude.

I could see the storm approaching with magnificent clouds stacked one on top of another, white and billowing, riding high against the azure sky. I couldn't see the terrain beneath the storm clouds from where I stood, but the air was now so hot that most of the rain the storm was dropping was evaporating before it hit the ground.

When a thunderstorm has spent its energy and any rain it carries, cool air drops vertically from the storm clouds toward the earth. When that air hits the earth, it begins to move horizontally, powering outflow winds that can exceed fifty miles per hour. These are the intense gusts you feel before a thunderstorm actually arrives. They're wild and they're unpredictable. When they hit an American suburb, say, in the Midwest, they blow leaves around, straighten flags on flagpoles, and topple a sign or two as they send people scurrying into their homes.

All wildland firefighters dread outflows and other wind events such as the passage of a cold front, the kind of wind event that spurred on the South Canyon Fire and killed fourteen firefighters.

We were all scanning the horizon, looking for any change of direction in the blaze and for flare-ups. When we spotted one, it was a race to see who could get on the radio first and report it. A little game of "beat the lookout at his own game." Jesse and I would call in and laugh if he pressed the button before I did.

It was almost a contest. It felt good to know that I was responding just as Jesse and Eric were. I felt I was seeing the fire as clear as day.

Maybe I am a good hotshot, I said to myself. *Maybe I'll be in Eric's league someday.*

CHAPTER TWENTY-FIVE

The fire fed on the afternoon heat. The rising winds fanned it like a bellows. It now spread across an approximately one to three mile front north and east of Yarnell. The fire had formed multiple active fronts. One local reporter later compared it to an octopus made out of flame. The flanks were each moving at different speeds, complicating the efforts to prioritize them.

At 2:13 p.m., officials approved the request for a Type 1 IMT to Yarnell. We were the only Arizona wildfire to get a Type 1 designation that day. Yarnell had now effectively been declared the most serious fire in the state.

By now, phones were ringing all over Yarnell: If the resident picked up, he or she heard a voice saying the Sheriff's Department was issuing a pre-evacuation bulletin. *Get ready to move* was the message. Emails popped up on cell phones saying the same thing.

There were more than four hundred men and women involved in the fight to save Yarnell and Peeples Valley. Multiple aircraft of different types plied the skies above the smoking hills. Six million gallons of water and two hundred thousand gallons of retardant would be dropped on the fire before day's end.

But the fire was proving unstoppable.

I watched as huge billows of dark smoke obscured the hill faces. Helitankers were etched black against the gray sky, their hoses hanging from their bellies like noxious insects. They were headed to Hidden Springs Ranch in Peeples Valley to refill with water. The VLATs swept down, parting the smoke in swirling tendrils that curled up on themselves.

Eric was still scouting the fire, heading north in the black. He was calling in what he was seeing, and by three p.m., I realized that he was parallel to me, though at a higher elevation.

When I saw a flare-up on the north side of the fire, I was about to thumb the radio when Eric called it in.

Words out of my mouth, I thought.

"Copy that," I said. I scanned the sky and saw that the storm clouds were moving closer.

At 3:26 p.m., the news darkened. The flaming front of the fire had doubled in size to three miles. Outflows from the storm were approaching the Yarnell Hill fire. And they'd swung around from the southwest to the west-northwest. The fire began to pivot ninety degrees. One flank of the fire heated up and began to run straight at Yarnell.

A supervisor reached Eric on the radio. Eric relayed that the lines of retardant dropped by the tankers had been compromised: The fire had burned right through them. The supervisor asked Eric if he could redeploy Granite Mountain into Yarnell, to try to save the town. The answer came back: negative. The crew was in the black. They were staying where they were.

For the next half hour, I did my weather reports and kept an eye on the storm cell. I didn't see the light-gray curtain that usually indicates rain from a distance. Rain would have been a godsend. But there was nothing in the enormous landscape I was studying except fuel and fire.

At about 3:50 p.m., Air Attack called Eric and reported that the fire was pushing toward Yarnell and could reach the town within one to two hours. The official warned Eric that the fire could overrun the Granite Mountain vehicle's current position. Eric copied that and said he was forming an escape plan for Granite Mountain. A supervisor on the ground checked in and asked Eric if he'd gotten the most recent weather update and if he was squared away. Eric confirmed he had.

"Okay, copy," the supervisor shot back. "Just keep me updated—you know, you guys hunker and be safe, and then we'll get some air support down there ASAP."

The curtain of smoke darkened to black and muddy brown. The fire was pushing across the ridges back to the south. It had now turned from a fairly ordinary high desert blaze into a firestorm.

The fire line became unstable. It had been pushing steadily northeast for many hours, but now the corkscrewing winds forced different sections of the fire in different directions. It was like dropping a heavy object onto a line of dominoes. The kinetic picture was becoming more extreme.

Fresh oxygen from the storm flowed into the fire and bloomed the flames wider, higher, and faster. Compounding the external gusts, a wildfire produces its own internal winds, which shoot heated water vapor vertically into the atmosphere (this is why pilots try not to fly over wildfires). These winds can also move horizontally at fantastic speeds that can rise to ten times the speed of the ambient gusts. The winds driving into the core of the Yarnell fire from the storm were now moving at forty to fifty miles per hour, but the winds inside the fire itself were moving much faster than that. Spotting became more intense as the gusts tossed embers in front of the wide arc of the firewall. New fires were springing up half a mile ahead, which then drew the main fire to them.

I could hear the crackle of the fire deepening into a roar. Heavy ash was falling on firefighters cutting firebreaks north of me. The dark-gray smoke laced with orange was now half a mile away from my flat rock and moving fast.

I could almost feel the fire in the air around me, how chokingly hot it was starting to get.

Around 3:45 p.m., the fire had reached the first trigger point set that morning by fire officials. The ridge one mile north of Yarnell was glowing orange. Supervisors ordered an immediate evacuation of all residents. A line of cars began to form on Route 89, crawling along in smoke so thick that it was impossible to see the next turn in the road. The Red Cross had by now set up a center in Prescott to care for the evacuating families.

The mind-set began to change almost imperceptibly from fighting the fire to escaping it.

It was around 3:52 p.m. The fire was moving northeast. I watched my trigger point, the drainage that sat three hundred yards away. I watched as the fire blew through it and began burning in the chaparral closer to me. I didn't anticipate it moving that fast.

If I didn't act quickly, my escape route would be cut off.

Radio problems were cropping up. One supervisor's air-to-ground frequency went out at 3:55 p.m., and the remaining channels grew thick with competing voices.

I got on our channel and told Jesse what I was seeing.

"I got eyes on you and the fire," he replied, "and it's making a good push."

I needed to relocate. I radioed that to Jesse.

"Copy that," Jesse said. "Donut, it's time to get out of there."

I didn't need to hear that twice. I quickly packed my weather kit and stuffed it into my pack. I told Jesse I was heading to the open space by the old dozer.

Jesse's voice was calm. "Okay, cool," he said.

I climbed down from the rock and headed into the green. The flames were behind me now, out of my line of sight, but I knew they were headed my way and gaining speed.

I walked quickly. *You left it too late*, I thought. *Go now.*

I hurried through the brush, heading for the old dozer. The roar of the fire was huffing behind me, growing louder and shriller.

If you make a mistake now, I thought, *that could be it. Call Blue Ridge. Get that UTV here.*

I was fighting back thoughts of burning up, of feeling the fire rush out at me from the brush around me. Not having eyes on the fire was the worst part. You feel like you're going to turn your head and the fire is going to come rushing at you through the trees with no warning. A wave that will burn you alive in three seconds.

I burst out of the brush at the clearing and brought the radio up to my mouth. I was going to call Brian, the Blue Ridge super. The dozer was there and I was about to hit the button for a pickup when I saw something rolling into the far edge of the clearing on fat black wheels.

I couldn't believe what I was seeing. Was it a mirage? I ran toward it, and saw it was the Blue Ridge UTV. I felt a huge weight lift off me. Brian Frisby had seen the flames moving toward me and had anticipated my need for a ride out—Eric had asked for a face-to-face meeting, so Brian swung by my position on the way. I hopped on and handed Brian the radio so he could talk directly to Jesse and Eric.

This guy just saved my life, I thought.

CHAPTER TWENTY-SIX

My experience was being replayed all over Yarnell. Five to seven minutes after reaching the first Yarnell trigger point, the fire blew through the second one. The distance between the two triggers was supposed to give firefighters ample time to evacuate the town in an orderly manner, but the process, in truth, had barely started by the time the flames broke through point number two. One supervisor would say later that if they had doubled the distances, they still wouldn't have given the crews and the locals adequate time to retreat. The fire was simply moving faster than anyone could remember a wildfire moving.

On the north end of Yarnell supervisors made sure the last of the firefighters were moving away from the firestorm. As they rounded up the final stragglers and headed south, they realized the light behind them had turned dark. They looked over their shoulders. The wall of black smoke was four stories high, blocking out the sun. Embers were dropping around them like black hail, tapping on their helmets and igniting tiny blazes that glowed like jack-o'-lanterns. The air became suffocating.

The UTV shot through the brush, heading downhill. Two minutes later I jumped off at the spot where the superintendent trucks were parked.

"If it gets hot, don't worry about the vehicles," Brian said. "Just move."

He needed to get drivers. Moving all our trucks out one at a time would take too long with just one or two guys. The fleet would burn up before I could do it myself.

I'd made it. Now my mind was on our vehicles. The thought that Granite Mountain might be in danger hadn't occurred to me; they were in the black, with good eyes on the fire. Eric and Jesse would take care of the others. There were decades of experience up there on that ridgeline.

On the radio, Jesse assured the Blue Ridge super that they were in the black and they were watching the fire. Eric was scouting the fire and other possible escape routes.

Everything was kosher. There was a plan.

Right about this time, up on that ridge, Chris MacKenzie picked up his cell phone and began shooting a video. In it, the boys are sitting in a field of granite boulders, the fire below them, a hot seam of lava-like orange. The crew is resting, adjusting their equipment and watching the fire that is ripping below them, sending billows of gray-brown smoke skyward. The mood on the video is relaxed but watchful; they're safe, their packs are on, there's chaw tucked into their cheeks, they're marveling a little at how the nothing fire has turned into a tempest. They're removed from the battle.

Eric's voice can be heard on the radio. "I was just saying that I knew this was coming when I called you, and I asked what your comfort level was. I could just feel it, y'know?"

He's talking to Jesse about the fire, how it's moving, how they both feel about what it's doing.

Jesse is nearby, out of frame. "I copy," he tells Eric. "And it's almost made it to that two-track road that we walked in on."

At that moment, Chris hit the stop button and the video ends. It's eighteen seconds long.

In another transmission to Jesse, Eric reported that the winds were turning "squirrely." It was, ironically, the same word a hotshot foreman had used on the South Canyon Fire nineteen years earlier, just minutes before the fire had chased down his crew and killed them.

At 3:54 p.m., another Granite Mountain hotshot texted a family member: *The fire is running at Yarnell!!!* From that ridge, there was nothing they could do to stop the fire.

All over the hills, everything changed in an instant. A captain of another group of firefighters was running through an arroyo, with rock walls on each side ten feet high, escaping as the sound of the fire echoed in the narrow canyons. When he looked up, he saw a dense river of gray smoke and a sheet of red fire over his head, jumping the gap between the rock walls. Without the stone that protected him, he would have been charred alive. He later estimated that had he waited just one minute more to move, he would have been caught in the inferno and incinerated.

I turned the volume on the radio up all the way so I could keep track of the fire. A supervisor was asking Blue Ridge if they had time to burn a backfire and slow the wildfire.

Negative, Blue Ridge responded.

Eric heard the report and his voice broke in. He said from his vantage point the fire had almost reached the buggies. He clearly had a good eye on the fire because it was very close.

The Blue Ridge guys and I were maneuvering the Granite Mountain trucks away from the flames, moving them to

Shrine Road. When we got there, I saw fire engines flying past, trying to cut off the fire before it completely engulfed the town. Later on there were houses on fire left and right, propane tanks shooting off in the near distance with eerie high-pitched whistles.

Yarnell was the focus. From what we knew, Granite Mountain was up above us, safe in the black.

At 4:04 p.m., up on the ridgeline, Wade took out his cell phone and snapped a picture of the fire—billowing tan-gray clouds shooting up into the atmosphere—and texted it to a family member: *This thing is running straight for yarnel [sic] just starting evac. You can see fire on left, town on right.*

The crew was now near where I'd left them, on the ridge where they'd set the backfires. They were heading southeast toward Boulder Springs Ranch, which Eric had picked out as the crew's safe zone that morning. Their route was along the two-track road, which wasn't a direct one; it curved around in a semicircle.

Around this time, I heard Eric's voice on the radio. Calm, deliberate. "I want to pass on that we're going to make our way to our escape route." My gut tightened.

"You guys are in the black, correct?" the Blue Ridge super shot back.

"Yeah, we're picking our way through the black . . . going out toward the ranch."

Blue Ridge super: "To confirm, you're talking about the road you saw me on with the UTV earlier, in the bottom?"

Eric again: "Yes, the road I saw you on with the Ranger." The conversation ended. The Boulder Springs Ranch, the bombproof area that Overhead had scouted that morning, was 1.3 miles away. Some believed they were moving toward it.

CHAPTER TWENTY-SEVEN

The fire was zero percent contained. It was bearing down on the northern part of Yarnell and burning everything in sight. I was hiking down Shrine Road with three other Blue Ridge hotshots when we got an urgent call from Brian on the radio.

"Get the trucks and get 'em out of there. Meet up at the Ranch House Restaurant."

I copied that and we headed toward the trucks. "Goddamn," I said, "they're pulling everyone out."

The town was quickly being engulfed. The fire's internal winds were shooting spot fires half a mile ahead. Fire was ahead of us and above us. We had this feeling of encirclement. The fire was burning through dozens of houses. Fire-eaten roofs crashed to the ground; walls collapsed in plumes of smoke, leaving door frames smoking in front of black ruins, fire licking at the char.

Around me, townspeople ran for their cars as the fire came into the town on hot sirocco winds. Houses in Yarnell were burning in strange, piecemeal patterns—one was completely burned out while the one next door was only singed.

Metal roofs melted into congealed globs of steel. Crystal glasses in cabinets bent and wilted in on themselves. Fire-fighters ran from door to door, yelling at people to get out.

The Blue Ridge hotshots and I pulled out of our position and began to make our way to safety. Other personnel were heading toward the restaurant, striving to get out of the fire's path. Some didn't want to leave. Supervisors jumped on their UTVs and zoomed along the dirt roads, shouting at the men to go. Now.

Cinders and smoke were choking the air. I could taste ash in my mouth with every breath. The evacuation was by now mandatory and immediate. Many people had left already, but any hotshot knows that it will amaze you how many people stay behind until the last moment. Some will fight you as you try to save them from certain death.

At 4:00 p.m., the outflow winds slammed into the fire's northern flank. The smoke on the fire line stiffened and rose up into a gray wall laced with pink-orange fire at its base. The fire turned on a dime, swerving away from the north and branching into several "heads" or flanks. It sprouted two fingers that turned and raced south and southeast. Even as the flames spread and covered a wider area, they were growing more intense. The fire was pumping a tremendous amount of brown-black smoke into the atmosphere. At 4:24 p.m., images on Doppler radar would show that the smoke plume had reached a height of about 31,500 feet, approaching the cruising altitude for commercial aircraft. By 4:33 p.m., the plume would climb to 38,700 feet.

There were intermittent dashes of rain. The crew members in the aircraft circling above, designated ASM2, noticed water mixing with ash on its windshield. They could hear thunder close by now, echoing in the cockpit before rumbling down to the terrain below. But little or no rain was reaching the fire.

Somewhere around 4:20 p.m., the crew of Granite Mountain reached a saddle of a ridge above a box canyon that was on the way to the Boulder Springs Ranch. They were on high ground with a clear view of the wildfire to the northeast. Between the ridge and the ranch was a box canyon, closed off on three sides by steep stone walls. It was filled with Gambel oak and manzanita.

In Yarnell, there was confusion about Granite Mountain's route. Brian Frisby assumed they were heading the other way—northeast toward other burned-over ranches that lay in the black. But Eric apparently wanted to stick to his original retreat spot, the "bombproof" one. Perhaps that earlier request to redeploy in Yarnell had influenced his thinking: Boulder Springs is closer to the town. Perhaps he wanted to be in position to help save what could be saved.

What was Eric thinking at this moment? Every supervisor is constantly balancing safety and aggressiveness. How can I keep my boys alive while also doing my job? How close to the fire is safe? If a supervisor always keeps his men far away from the fire line, eventually forest and homes will burn. He will defeat the purpose of his crew. He might lose his job.

Eric was calculating time, distance, wind speed, relative humidity, and fuel type and putting those numbers through twenty years of experience fighting wildfires. From the top of the ridge, the canyon appeared to be a straight shot to the ranch. There was a wash to the right where water had cleared out a pale gash and very little vegetation grew, but it's unclear whether Eric or Jesse spotted it.

The radios were choked with voices and static. I was trying to keep track of Granite Mountain's movement. But there was only silence from them. As the Blue Ridge guys and I scrambled to move their trucks, the eighteen Granite Mountain crew members were on the saddle of the ridge.

Then the crew moved down from the saddle into the box canyon. They had to cut their way through tangled brush. Their saws were revving. As soon as they descended deeper into the chaparral, their view of the fire would have been obscured, and by the time they were approaching the floor of the canyon, it would have been blocked by the ridge wall to their left. Maybe they saw the smoke standing straight up like a cloak hanging on a hook. But that was it.

When you drop into a box canyon or into high scrub, you lose essential information about the fire: You can't feel the wind speed on your face anymore. The canyon walls protect you from that. You can't see what the fire's doing. You can see the smoke wall, but that is a lagging indicator, often indicating a change in fire direction several minutes after it happens. Deep in the chaparral, you become blind to the flaming front.

Hovering over the fire was ASM2, a second fixed-wing aircraft that had relieved the first one on the scene, which had finished its shift at 2:27 p.m. ASM2 was now coordinating the air response to the fire. (The pilot of the Air Attack fixed-wing aircraft had timed out on the number of hours he was allowed to fly, and left the area at around 4:00 p.m.) In the cockpit, the pilot was telling incoming air tankers where to drop their loads when he heard a snippet on the radio while another crew member was talking with fire supervisors on the air-to-ground frequency. Suddenly, this crew member cut in. "I heard a crew in a safety zone. Do we need to call a time-out?" He wanted to know if the aircraft should abandon firefighting to do flyovers and check on the hotshot crew. A supervisor radioed back. "No, they're in a good place. They're safe and it's Granite Mountain."

The crew was making their way down into the box canyon by this time, bushwhacking through thick foliage. They had stepped out of the black and into the green. Some who'd been following their transmissions believed they were on the black ridge, but in fact they'd left it minutes before and their progress down into the canyon made a retreat back to the blackened two-track increasingly unfeasible.

Suddenly, Eric was on the radio: "We're going down our escape route to our safety zone."

"Is everything okay?" the supervisor says.

"Yes, we're just moving."

Eric didn't indicate that the crew had moved off the black and into the box canyon. His voice sounded normal.

At 4:20 p.m., the outflow winds from the thunderstorm swept down from the clouds and slammed into the southern edge of the blaze. The fire now exploded and instantly turned another ninety degrees. The wall of flame was now perhaps one hundred feet at its highest. And it was moving along a new route. Just after Granite Mountain had lost sight of the fire, the fire pivoted directly at them.

The eighteen men making their way through brush that reached over their heads were completely unaware of what had happened.

The fire picked up speed. It whipped through the dry brush, carried by winds gusting to fifty miles per hour. One local later described the fire now as "both moving and flying," so impatient to consume what was ahead of it that it had lifted from the ground and inhabited the desert air.

The human body is no match for these conditions. A body taking two consecutive breaths of three-hundred-degree air will die within seconds. Driven by cold downdrafts, the fire was sucking in the crisp new oxygen and was now burning at two thousand degrees.

A few minutes later, the flames reached the last trigger point, the final ridge before the town proper began. A supervisor made a hurried call to Air Attack.

"Drop at will!" he called into the radio. The DC-10s screamed overhead, dropping low to try to save the town, dumping thousands of gallons of retardant where the flames were biggest. Granite Mountain was now the only crew still in the hills; everyone else was retreating toward Route 89 or trying to get out of the fire's way.

We were driving toward the restaurant on Route 89. I spotted the place, with its wide parking lot cleared of brush, with no scrub oak to burn. As I pulled into the lot, I saw firefighters sitting on the ground, spent, and old people laid out on stretchers.

The focus was on saving Yarnell and not getting burned up ourselves.

In the town, the firestorm continued to rage. Branches and knifelike embers shot through the air, alighting on roofs and shattering windows. Those windows that weren't broken melted in the heat. In the unburned section, the wind was bending the trees, turning their leaves over from green to silver and making a sound like water shooting through narrow rapids.

At 4:37 p.m., Eric looked up and saw a DC-10 airplane flying east to west, preparing to drop its retardant. "That's exactly what we're looking for," he radioed the pilot. "That's where we want the retardant." But by the time the tanker turned for its drop, the winds had shifted and the hill was shrouded in smoke. The pilot aborted the run. The hill below the pilot was now a roiling carpet of black and gray.

By this point, the fire was ripping across the ridge to Granite Mountain's left. The canyon itself acted as a heat trap, allowing no escape for the smoke or fire that were beginning to pour through the brush. Chaparral and manzanita exploded before the flames even reached them. On the shoulders of the nearby hills, great granite boulders that have acted as sentinels for millennia burst their skins from the intense heat, shedding basketball-sized flakes of stone.

The fire was moving down into the canyon at about thirteen miles per hour. The average human being can run for short distances at a top speed of fifteen miles per hour. But that is unencumbered by packs and along a clear, flat path. The men at the floor of the canyon were wearing heavy gear and thick-soled leather boots and were caught in a place with no clear egress. If they'd spotted the wash to their right and dropped their packs, perhaps they could have outrun the flames. It would have been a very close race. But there is no evidence that they saw the wash.

Somewhere between 4:37 and 4:39 p.m., the situation changed drastically. The radio was thick with voices. Everyone was calling in homes that were endangered or blazing up. At 4:39, I was sitting in the truck when I heard a Granite Mountain crew member's voice struggling through the static: "*Breaking in on Arizona Sixteen, Granite Mountain Hotshots, we are in front of the flaming front.*"

My heart froze. I'd never heard Eric's voice like this— panicked, anguished. And the words "*in front of the flaming front.*" How was that even possible? Granite Mountain was supposed to be in the cold black, up on a ridge, with acres of black behind them. Untouchable. How could the wall of fire have caught them?

The transmission caused confusion in Yarnell. "Is Granite Mountain still in there?" a firefighter listening to the transmissions called out.

"Well, they're in a safety zone," another answered. "In the black."

The fire must have appeared over the ridge to Granite Mountain's left. It had also cut off the canyon's mouth ahead of them. The escape route to the ranch was disappearing. There might have been a small opening to the west, hard by the canyon wall, but the flames were closing it quickly.

The fire had appeared out of nowhere, five stories high. To be caught in grasslands in front of a moving fire is something to be dreaded. But at least you can run. To face a voracious fire in a bramble of trees and scrub, unable to move three feet without encountering an obstacle, is simply terrifying.

Firefighters moving toward the safety of Route 89 stopped what they were doing and listened to the radio. They thought about the chainsaws audible in the background of Eric's transmission. Why would a team retreating to a safety zone along a cold black trail be cutting with saws? That burring sound over the radio was a confirmation that Granite Mountain was not in the black—where there was no flammable brush to cut. They were in the green.

"I hear saws running," said a firefighter listening in. "That's not good."

A voice broke in on the radio.

It was an unidentified member of Granite Mountain.

A supervisor responded: "Granite Mountain, Operations on air-to-ground."

A few seconds later, a panicked voice: *"Air Attack, Granite Mountain Seven, how do you copy me?"*

No rescue team could reach nineteen men in a box canyon with a wildfire bearing down on them. The only hope for relief was from the air: If a tanker could spot the crew and lay a line of retardant over them, it might buy them a little time. So Eric was calling to Air Attack, presumably to ask for a drop. But ASM2 thought Granite Mountain was in the black and safe.

Granite Mountain was back on the radio: *"Air Attack, Granite Mountain Seven!"* He was yelling now. The pilot—unaware of what was happening—cut in and told him to stop shouting. Another firefighter said, "That's not good."

"No, he's screaming," another agreed.

A supervisor called to the pilot. "Okay, Granite Mountain Seven sounds like they got some trouble. Uh, go ahead and get that, he's trying to get you on the radio, let's go ahead and see what we've got going on."

The pilot copied that.

Before he could call Granite Mountain, Eric was back. His voice was calmer. "Division Alpha with Granite Mountain." He was still trying to establish contact.

The pilot called back, "Okay, uh, Division Alpha."

In the two or three seconds that elapsed with the pilot's response, something changed again. Eric's voice was again bordering on shouting. Saws were ripping in the background. "Yeah, I'm here with Granite Mountain Hotshots, our escape route has been cut off. We are preparing a deployment site and we are burning out around ourselves in the brush and I'll give you a call when we are under the sh-shelters."

I felt sick. *This cannot be happening*, I thought. I wanted to scream into the radio.

Granite Mountain had realized by then that they couldn't make the ranch.

I was speechless. I felt as if my nightmare from the Doce Fire—of being trapped by intense flames—was coming true. But it was happening to my brothers.

In the canyon, the hotshots were cutting in a crude circle while swampers rushed to drag the brush to the perimeter and throw it as far as they could. Guys were running at the edge of the circle, dripping fire onto the brush, trying to burn out a ring around themselves. As the fire roared a hundred feet high and they knew it was seconds from blowing through the circle, they heaved back and threw their saws deep into the thick brush. The small amount of oil inside the saws, if ignited, would add only a tiny fraction of heat to the firestorm that was as big as an apartment block. But this is what they were trained to do. Their minds were being starved of oxygen, confused by toxic fumes pushed ahead of the flames.

The pilot copied. "So you're on the south side of the fire, then?"

At 4:42, Eric: *"AFFIRM!"*

The canyon must have been a swirling storm of cinders, smoke, and airborne poisons.

"'Kay," the pilot shot back, "we're gonna bring you the VLAT, okay?"

The pilot asked the VLAT to come to the southeast and orbit until he could see Granite Mountain and direct the drop. The VLAT pilot copied that and said he would keep "full eyes" on ASM2 and be ready to dump his load to help Granite Mountain. He was circling the burning hills, waiting for the drop coordinates.

If he hit them directly, perhaps they would have had a chance. Or if he had dropped the retardant on the fire line just in front of them, perhaps he could have bought them seconds. A minute, perhaps. But the fire was so powerful now that it was basically impervious to chemicals or water or any human endeavor to stop it.

The pilots in the various aircraft flying over Yarnell struggled to make out the terrain below them. Plumes of black smoke were funneling up past their windshields as if they were inside a burning silo. They knew that below them somewhere was Granite Mountain. But where in the swirling blackness were the missing hotshots? One of the pilots tilted his rotors and peered down through the cinders and ash. They reported extreme fire behavior and heavy smoke on the landscape below.

The hotshots now stripped themselves of their packs. The fire was roaring like jet engines at full throttle. Manzanita and scrub oak detonated with showers of ash and bark. The men's lungs strained for breathable air. They ripped the tightly rolled shelters from their packs, flung them out, and fell to the dusty ground, catching their handmade boots inside the silver foil and stretching out. They couldn't hear each other with the shrieking of the inferno. The temperature soared hundreds of degrees in a matter of seconds as the flaming wall approached.

They were in front of the inferno now, crouching at its feet. The air turned poisonous and unbearably hot. Their last chance was to stay under the shelters and hope that the fire blew over them without too much damage to the fragile bodies underneath.

No one had run. They were close enough to touch each other. Their voices, if they were yelling, were drowned in the deep-throated roar of the fire. Under the darkness of the smoke plume, the circle around them brightened and the shelters, their foil rippling away in the wind that raced ahead of the fire, reflected the orange of the dancing flames.

The men turned their heads away from the super-heated air. Those inside the shelters grabbed the edges of the foil and tried to force them down, trying to keep the toxic air and the flames from boiling into the tent, as the blisteringly hot gases shot past, rocking the shelters. They turned their faces to the earth and sucked in a breath. Carbon monoxide poured into the shelters, dizzying the men and clouding their brains. If they inhaled enough of it, what was happening all around would have appeared to be a dream or a form of derangement.

The fire was now seven stories high. It was hot enough to burn uranium. It swept through the scrub oak and pine, the branches making a tiny clicking noise in the deafening roar. The winds took the flames and bent them close to the earth, which increased the fire's intensity. The terrain around the men appeared to explode into daylight.

The fire fell on them.

CHAPTER TWENTY-EIGHT

A bove the canyon, the pilot of Helicopter 215KA was sitting at a helibase preparing to go refuel. But then he heard Eric's final transmissions. He immediately lifted off and radioed ASM2; they both began prowling over the flaming hills, looking for Granite Mountain. The smoke over the box canyon was so heavy by now that neither crew could see through to the ground.

The pilot: "Granite Mountain, do you copy?"

Static blared on the radio. Someone was thumbing the mic on his radio but uttering no sound.

"We're working our way around there," the pilot called. "We've got several aircraft coming to you. We'll see if we can't take care of business for you."

No response.

"I need you to pay attention," the pilot said, "and tell me when you hear the aircraft, okay? 'Cause it's gonna be a little tough for us to see you." With visuals gone, they would try to home in on Granite Mountain's position by sound.

Granite Mountain's radio clicked again and stayed down. The channel was open at their end and broadcasting. There was a loud pulsing sound, like a hammer hitting a length of sheet metal, but no voices. There was also the sound of rushing air, which must have been the firestorm moving across the canyon.

The pilot: "Division Alpha, Bravo Three Three, do you hear a helicopter?"

Three fast clicks on the radio. Someone in Granite Mountain was hitting the transmit button but not saying anything.

At Boulder Springs Ranch, the "bombproof" safety zone that the fire supervisors had identified that morning, the owner was unaware of what was happening in the box canyon a couple hundred yards from her front door. She walked out of the handsome wooden home to check on her dog, who was roaming around outside. She looked to her left and saw a black wall of smoke hemmed by hot flame roaring toward the ranch. She yelled to her husband and ran for the pen where her numerous animals were exposed. Her husband dashed to the barn, throwing open the door. With the roar of the fire concussing the air, the two herded their animals into the barn and shut the door. They raced back to their home. They weren't inside more than a minute when the fire rushed over the ranch and began burning to the south.

Their home and the barn were unharmed. Having built with fire-resistant materials and scrupulously cleared the grounds of brush, the owners and their animals survived. The ranch had indeed proved to be bombproof.

At the restaurant, I could see the ridge of the box canyon. We were all watching the brown and black smoke coiling and twisting as flames surged up the slope. Finally the fire gained the top of the ridge and shot 150 feet in the air. I felt nauseous. If Granite Mountain was anywhere near that . . . I didn't finish the thought.

I was trying to keep the dark thoughts at bay. *They got out*, I kept telling myself. *They dropped their radios but they made it. I'll see them soon.*

Voices on the radio.

"Operations, Three Three, any communication yet?"

"No, negative, Tanker Nine One Zero thought she heard him but I've been unable to get anything."

"Do you have any firm location where they're at?"

"No . . . I would say the southeast corner of the fire. That's the best I can do for you right now."

In Yarnell proper, it was as dark as if night had settled overhead. Security cameras sensed the alteration in light and changed from day to night mode. Vehicles moving out to Route 89 switched on their headlights to see through the drafts of smoke and embers. The emergency lights of ambulances flashed as they carried bewildered residents toward open spaces. The faces in the windows looked pale, shocked.

It was just chaos now. No order. You didn't know where the fire was; you had the feeling that you could turn a corner and it would spring at you from a line of brush, coming at you faster than you could run, and you'd be done. Nowhere was safe.

Time started to break down. Or perhaps it was my grip on it. I was waiting for my brothers to come trudging down the road, their faces caked with smoke residue, their white teeth showing through the black.

I started talking to God in my mind. I asked him to take me and let my friends survive. I would have gladly lain down in the flames at that moment if it meant my brothers could live.

Other firefighters began to measure time by the last call from Granite Mountain.

"How long's it been?" one called to another.

"Thirty minutes?"

Fire officials initiated a medical response. They asked five paramedics and three EMTs who were stranded at the restaurant to make themselves ready. They issued a call for five medevac helicopters. They set up a triage center and notified a nearby burn unit that they might be getting injured patients from Yarnell.

I was running around scrounging up medical supplies and getting them ready for when Granite Mountain came in. They might be burned; they might need oxygen for their scarred lungs. I wanted to be ready for them. Once I'd gotten all the stuff, I monitored the radios and prayed for Jesse or Eric to say they were all right.

The fire was still raging, but Brian Frisby and Rogers Trueheart Brown, Blue Ridge's crew captain, decided to go in on the UTVs. I helped them get their gear together and when they were ready, I went up to Brian. "Bring 'em back," I said. "Please bring my brothers back."

He nodded. Brian and Rogers jumped on a UTV and Brian revved it up, then put it into gear. Other firefighters, hearing about the deployment on the radio, rushed to join them. Supervisors were repeatedly trying to raise Eric on the radio, but there was only silence. Not even static or clicking.

The UTVs zigzagged through Yarnell on their way to the two-track road. They drove through the outskirts of the town, into a pall of light-gray smoke lit by orange spot fires to their left and right. Burned-out homes showed as a series of blackened rectangles—door frames all that was left of the structures. Trucks in their driveways tottered on melted tires. The air was still choking hot and burned tree limbs crunched beneath the UTVs' wheels. The hotshots probed ahead, calling to each other to watch the power lines, which sagged in the heat. At times it seemed like the fire ahead was not the remnants of the fire wall but a flank of it, sweeping around for another run through town.

"Fuck it," one firefighter cried. "Let's go for it."

They found a dirt track. Their engines growled and the tires thudded on the rutted road as they made their way upslope. Palls of tan-gray smoke. There was less fire out there than in the town.

The crew of a helicopter known as Ranger 58 heard the radio traffic and loaded medical gear into the cabin before taking off at 5:16 p.m. They flew to the last reported position of Granite Mountain and hovered over the smoke-enshrouded hill. They spotted what looked like a backpack pump—a portable five gallon water bag and nozzle used by firefighters during suppression. They reported their finding on the radio. Did it belong to Eric?

They asked me over the radio if Granite Mountain carried backpack pumps. "No, we didn't have them today," I said. It had to be from someone else. "Any idea where they are?"

I told them the crew should have been on the two-track going toward Boulder Springs, unless they'd broken off and headed north toward the other ranches in the black.

The radio buzzed with static.

"Can you give me the names of everyone with them?"

I started to recite the names of my brothers.

The UTVs threaded their way up a path cleared by a dozer. Everything around them was blasted and smoking.

When the trail ran out, they dismounted and walked across the tops of canyon ridges, the scene in front of them peaceful now, the pale smoke from the fire lying in the valleys like morning mist, with only the ancient rocky spurs of the hills visible. The men themselves were nowhere in sight.

"Come on, Granite," one of the firefighters called out, "let's hear you talk."

The Ranger 58 pilot turned his craft toward Boulder Springs Ranch. He'd recalled the earlier transmission: Granite Mountain had set this ranch as their safety zone. At 6:10 p.m., the smoke was slowly clearing and the pilot spotted something glinting down below. He realized it was a series of deployment shelters located on the floor of a box canyon. From above, the canyon looked "moonscaped," everything except stone and hardy tree branches carbonized by the firestorm. The pilot got on the radio and called in the location. The canyon lay approximately one mile south-southeast of Granite's last reported position.

The pilot brought his helicopter down and landed five hundred yards away from the shelters, which were being tugged across the ground by a light breeze. Eric Tarr, the flight medic, grabbed a first-aid bag and jumped out. He marched toward the shelters, talking into a radio clipped to his shoulder. The landscape was something out of a Brothers Grimm forest: partially exploded granite boulders sat alongside blackened, twisted manzanita branches. The fire was moving so fast when it came through that it didn't have time to burn the trees themselves. Nothing green had been left behind. The ground was smoking.

Tarr had a water tube connected to a backpack and he sipped on it as he walked, trying to alleviate the terrific heat. Suddenly, he heard voices up ahead. He was stunned.

It seemed inconceivable that anything could have survived what had just come through this canyon, but Tarr quickened his pace to reach the shelters. The foil was glinting and moving in the wind like silvery fish flitting through black water. Tarr called out.

As he reached the deployment zone, Tarr saw bodies laid out on the ground in a twenty-four-by-thirty-foot space, arrayed in a rough horseshoe. Seven of the hotshots were still inside their shelters. The voices he'd heard came from Granite Mountain's radios, which were scattered on the ground. Somehow the radios had survived the flames.

Everyone at the restaurant had stopped to listen.

"Yeah, Todd," Tarr said over the radio. "On scene. Eighteen confirmed." He'd miscounted by one. There were actually nineteen bodies.

Boulder Springs Ranch lay six hundred yards away.

I was sitting in one of the Granite Mountain buggies. A cell phone went off behind me. I looked back. Then another. I knew the news of the tragedy was just filtering out into Prescott, and the families of the nineteen men were calling their loved ones to find out if they were safe. Each ping represented a mother or a wife or a father or brother hoping a voice they knew would answer.

I didn't know what to do. I got out of the buggy and walked down the road until I couldn't hear the phones' chirping anymore.

CHAPTER TWENTY-NINE

Someone drove me from the restaurant to the incident command post that had been set up about a mile away. The first face I saw was that of Tony Sciacca, the guy who first encouraged me to get into hotshotting. Alongside him was my teacher from the Fire Explorers. When I saw them I started crying, and once I started, I couldn't stop.

I was asking myself what everyone must have been thinking: Why had I made it out when my crew hadn't? I tried to go back and retrace my steps and the crew's steps and where each of them intersected with the blaze, but my mind locked up. I could only feel the sorrow sludging up my heart.

Someone, I forget who, said I had to go somewhere and give an after-incident report—a debriefing on what you know and what you saw. It's standard when a hotshot gets hurt out in the wild. I nodded. I would do it. Whatever I could do.

I felt an arm across my shoulder. It was Tony. His eyes were veined with red and he looked at me.

"Just go home to your mom."

A fire chief from Prescott volunteered to drive me home. But as I got my stuff together, he received a call on his cell: Granite Mountain families were gathering at a local school. That was going to be their rendezvous point.

"Take me there," I said to the chief.

He sighed.

"You sure you want to do that, Brendan?"

I told him I did.

We got in his truck. It took an hour to drive to the school. I don't remember much about the ride. Any thought I had, anything at all—*This is that country song that Michaela likes* or something like that—would instantly be overtaken by a rush of dread. *But they're dead. They're dead. What does it matter what song is playing?* There was no room in my mind for anything but raw grief. It was a horrible, claustrophobic feeling. It said, *You will never have another thought, or another emotion, that isn't touched by these nineteen deaths.*

We pulled up in front of the school and got out. I was dreading what was coming but I felt I had to be there. If I could help even one family member just a little bit, it would be worth it. My feelings were beside the point. I knew if something had happened to me, Chris and Eric and Travis would have done anything for my family.

I walked in. There was a buzz of conversation and I heard it dip. I saw a couple of guys I knew, guys I'd worked with. On their faces I could see bewilderment. They looked at me and I heard them through the buzz. "Dude, I am so sorry." "Brendan, are you okay?"

What could I say? It was embarrassing to be getting anyone's sympathy. I wasn't hurt. I had no wounds on me; my yellows weren't singed by smoke. I almost wished I had some injury that would have shown that I tried to save the guys. But there was nothing. I was obscenely healthy.

The tears came again. Then I saw a family member—one of the mothers—approaching. She took my arm and held it gently.

"Brendan, what happened?" she said.

I was shell-shocked. A black wave of guilt washed over me.

"I don't know. I'm so sorry. I don't know what happened."

More family members gathered around. I could guess what they wanted to hear. Specifics. "It was a fluke gust" or "The radios were out." But there was no one factor to point to.

I spent the evening at the school, hugging the wives and sisters and daughters and the brothers and fathers and uncles. I felt the urge to leave, to run away and go to my mom's house and curl up on my bed. Turn off the lights. But my place was here with the families.

We were all numb with disbelief.

That night I stayed at my mom's place. Some close friends from outside Granite Mountain came over and talked with me, but I was still in shock and didn't have much to say. The next morning I went back to my apartment. Chris's stuff was where he'd left it the morning before. His favorite beer was in the fridge. The rooms were so still.

I walked into Chris's bedroom and looked around. I could still sense his presence. I felt as though he was going to come in right after me and slap me on the back. "What are you crying for, bitch?" And we'd laugh and he'd go to the fridge and get a couple of beers, and life would start up again. That life looked so good to me now. Just to have Chris back. Just shooting the shit. Eating pizza and playing video games. That would have been everything.

But as it was I just lay on his bed. I started sobbing, covered my face with my hands. He wasn't coming back. None of them were.

I don't know how long I spent there. After a while, I had to take a piss, so I got up and went to the bathroom. I reached for the doorknob, but when I looked down my hand was shaking. I tried to grip the knob but my hand was flailing up and down so bad I couldn't get my fingers on the metal. I was staring at it through my tears.

"What is going on? What the f—"

I stepped back and felt rage take me over. I lifted my foot and slammed it into the bathroom door. It shot back and ricocheted off the bathroom wall, then bounced back a couple of feet and shivered on its hinges. The noise echoed in the empty apartment behind me.

It felt good to kick that thing.

I stepped forward and drove my foot into the bottom of the door again. It sprang back. I kicked it again, harder. I thought, *Yeah, that's it. Keep going. Break it and then kick every fucking thing in this apartment until it shatters.*

But the rage died away in a second. I felt numb again.

I went back to the school the next morning. I just wanted to be of service. I would have given anything to have comforted just one of the family members.

Instead, people were trying to comfort me. The owner of the rental property company for my apartment, a retired fireman, called me that evening and, after a few minutes of awkward conversation, said, "Listen. Don't worry about the rent for the next few months, okay?" I thanked him.

I went into town to my favorite Italian place and the check was picked up, by whom I don't know. For months, I would not pay for a meal. I would not pay for dry-cleaning, for takeout Chinese, for a car wash. I would not pay for anything. I tried to. But the people of Prescott wouldn't let me.

I needed that love. I realize that now. But at the time, it was so difficult to accept it. A lump would rise in my throat and my eyes would burn and I would mumble, "Thank you." The people who did those things will never know how much they meant to me. It felt like the town was lifting me up on its shoulders and saying, "We'll never let you fall, Brendan."

But at the same time, I felt unworthy. My brothers were gone and I was getting all this free shit. It was so wrong it was almost funny. I tried to be what I thought people needed me to be: strong. I'm sure if someone looked in my eyes they caught a glimpse of sadness and desolation, but I tried my best to hide it.

Who was I to say I was hurting?

The bodies of my brothers had been taken directly from Yarnell to the medical examiner's office in Phoenix. Seven days after the tragedy, we went to Phoenix to retrieve the bodies of the nineteen and bring them back to Prescott. There was a huge procession of cars—police, forest service, state patrol—led by cops on their motorcycles. Biker gangs from the area drove in ranks of big Harleys. I rode in the Granite Mountain superintendent's truck—Eric's old vehicle—alongside Chief Darrell Willis and Chief Ralph Lucas from the Prescott Fire Department. All I could manage to do was look out the window and stare at the landscape.

We went to the Phoenix mortuary, loaded the bodies into hearses, and set off across the desert. The fire in Yarnell was still burning, but the crews came off the fire line and stood by the side of the road, their helmets off, saluting. I looked up and saw people crowded onto the highway overpasses, standing in front of their fire trucks. Utility trucks with their booms extended and big American flags hanging off them. Masses of people everywhere. We drove through the towns and little villages on the way to Prescott and saw people standing on the side of the road, the men with their cowboy hats held to their chests, the women with hands up to cover their mouths in grief. I had to look away.

I remember we drove past the ranch where the parents of Travis Carter, one of the hotshots, lived. His dad was standing by the road, just waiting by the black asphalt, his head bowed. I wondered if he knew which hearse carried his son. We stopped the truck, got out, and hugged his dad, tears in our eyes.

When we got to Prescott, the roads were choked with people. The whole town pretty much shut down. We drove by them to the mortuary. My heart was heavy and tears rolled down my face.

At the mortuary, I got out and helped unload the bodies of my brothers. I'd expected they would be in caskets, but to my shock, they were in orange body bags, some of them covered with American flags and each one marked with the name of the man inside. The hearse would pull up and a voice would call out the name of the man inside, and I helped carry him into the mortuary freezer, my face expressionless.

I could feel their bodies through the orange plastic. My hands touched their heads, their legs, their arms. Some of the flags had blood on them and some of the bags were partially unzipped.

I'm not sure whose body it was, but one of the bags was unzipped near the bottom and I could see inside. It was one of my brothers' legs, and I thought, *Why is it covered in dirt?* But it wasn't dirt, of course. It was his skin, burned the color of mahogany. I cried and I took the zipper and pushed it all the way down so no one else would see. I was just sick inside.

After all the bodies were loaded into the mortuary freezer, we prayed over them with a pastor, who asked God to accept them into His arms. Afterward, the pastor asked me if I wanted some time alone and I said yes, I did. The others slowly made their way to the exit. I looked at the bags, trying to visualize the faces of the men inside. I wanted to know what my brothers looked like, but I was afraid to unzip the bags. I wanted to know their condition, but I didn't want to know.

I felt this wave of loneliness, of wrongness. *Why am I not in one of these bags? Why was I left here without you guys?*

I walked down the line and touched each of my brothers on the leg, feeling them through the plastic. *I love you*, I said to each one. *I'm so sorry I couldn't have been with you and helped you in your last moments.* I said good-bye.

Then I walked out into the hot sunshine. There were clusters of firefighters outside. Bottles appeared, whiskey and bourbon. We passed them around and drank toasts to the men inside.

CHAPTER THIRTY

My picture was in the paper and on the local news, and suddenly everyone knew my face. Sometimes people would see me and start to cry, and I'd cry, too.

Your mind plays tricks on you. Weird ones. I'd walk through town and I'd think I could hear what people were saying as they spotted me. You have strange thoughts about even being outside, going for milk or something. *Do people think I came out to feel their sympathy? Does it look like I'm going out just to get noticed? Should I become a hermit?*

Eventually I grew a beard. It helped a little. But then people recognized the beard.

I'd never wanted to be known as a victim of anything. Just the opposite. I'd been a victim of my family history and my own bad choices my whole life. Granite Mountain gave me the chance to be something else: a hardworking, responsible man. Someone in charge of his own life, someone willing to give to others. A strong person. Now, at twenty-one, I was something very different: the lone survivor.

What good is it being famous for making it out alive of

something that killed your best friends? It's like a negative fame. You're famous for something you didn't do. Die. It's harsh, but that's the honest truth.

Everywhere I went was for a funeral or a memorial or some event connected to Yarnell. I just wanted to get away, be anonymous, but that wasn't possible. A few weeks or so after the tragedy, I was scheduled to fly to New York to appear on *Good Morning America*. When I got to the Phoenix airport for my flight, the TSA employees saw me in the security line and waved me forward. I was thinking, *I appreciate y'all but I'll just stay right here, thank you all the same*. But they were being gracious, they wanted to show me love, and so I went forward and skipped the long line. I could imagine the other travelers saying, "Wait, isn't that Brendan McDonough?"

Even in Manhattan people knew who I was, believe it or not. I was walking down Madison Avenue and a woman saw me. "Aren't you that kid, that firefighter or something?" she said. I couldn't believe it. Every time I was recognized it brought back the faces of Chris and the others. Made the pain fresh again.

It wasn't a normal grieving process. I didn't stay in my room and just cry my heart out. I felt it was my job to go to every funeral I could, speak at every memorial, attend every fund-raiser, do every interview. It was my job to protect the families in any way possible. If I wasn't going to do TV interviews, someone was going to bug a wife or a mother to do them. Officials of the city of Prescott and their fire department asked me to do some interviews, and I obliged.

I felt responsible for my brothers' families, for their kids, too. I said to myself, *I need to be there to help their sons and daughters. If I'd died, Chris and the others would have taken care of Michaela, made sure she was all right.* But how could I lessen their pain?

I wanted to use myself up in helping these people, but I didn't know where to start.

There were so many dark moments. After the tragedy and the outpouring of love came the questions. *Why would nineteen experienced hotshots go down into a green canyon with a flaming front nearby? Somebody isn't telling the whole truth.* Reporters ran around asking anyone even remotely connected with the fire what had really happened. There were rumors, tons of them. I started to hear words like "cover-up" and "conspiracy." And then the lawsuits started.

In December, the Arizona Division of Occupational Safety and Health released its report on the fire. It was a bombshell. It reported that the first incident commander at Yarnell, the guy in charge of fighting the fire, had been exhausted and had worked twenty-eight days straight, possibly compromising his decision making. It said that the Arizona State Forestry Division ignored its own safety guidelines and failed to recognize that, in light of the extreme fire behavior being exhibited that day, their tactics "could not succeed." Officials had pursued a strategy that put "protection of non-defensible structures and pastureland over firefighter safety." It said that officials knew the strategy wasn't working and were aware that a storm was going to push the flames toward the nineteen men, but failed to pull them off the line in time. It also said that I and a bunch of other hotshots were "exposed to possible smoke inhalation, burns and death." They levied a fine of $559,000 for mishandling the fire and putting firefighters, including Granite Mountain, in danger. State Forestry appealed the fine.

You could feel the mood of Prescott start to change. It always does when experts and lawyers get involved. What happened at Yarnell was so inexplicable and mysterious that someone must be hiding something. Clearly. And I was the only hotshot standing, so I became the object of a good deal of gossip.

The questions had an edge to them now. "What *really* happened out there, Brendan? Huh? What aren't you telling us? And why?"

Left unsaid was *Why didn't you save those guys?* I asked myself that all the time. *Why didn't you do more? Were you emphatic enough in telling the guys that the fire was turning? Could you have warned them somehow in those critical moments around 4:20 p.m.?*

But to say, "Eric, this thing is moving fast, stay in the black" never even occurred to me; it would have been a waste of my breath. Eric was our leader. He knew what he was doing. If I'd had specific information he lacked, I would have transmitted it immediately. But we were seeing the same things. And I didn't know half as much as he'd forgotten during his career.

There was another voice inside my head, playing devil's advocate. *What could you have done, exactly? Stayed at your position and burned to death? For what?* That still wouldn't have saved the other guys. All I would have done would have been to add another name to the memorials and break a few more hearts. Nothing else would have changed.

In the small part of my mind that was still capable of rational thought, I knew this was true. Every scenario I dreamed up for saving the crew shared one thing: They were all completely unrealistic. I couldn't have stopped what happened. All I could do was stop it from taking one more victim.

But the first voice, the voice of guilt and rage, was stronger. I'd failed. I was the reason that so many lives around me were filled with pain. And I found that hard to take.

One of the lowest times came when I heard that a relative of one of the Granite Mountain guys said I must have been drunk or on drugs the day of the tragedy. At the same time, another family member said authorities were covering up what really happened at Yarnell and I was part of the conspiracy. I couldn't believe it. I'd been out the night before the tragedy having a few cocktails, sure, but that was typical for a lot of guys on the crew. Drinking the day of a job, when our lives were at risk? Being drunk on the fire line? No way. I was speechless. There were accusations that I was hiding what had really happened, as part of some kind of government cover-up. Another dagger that went deep.

I brooded about those two things for months. How could family members think that of me? I knew these people. I'd tried to protect them after the tragedy. I'd stood up for their loved ones as best I could.

I got angry. I smashed some shit at my apartment. More than once. Because of the lawsuits, many of which were going to call me as a witness, I couldn't respond to the accusations. My depression found new depths to sink to.

I felt like I was being attacked just for surviving. It seemed as if I'd be tangled up in lawsuits for years to come. I had no problem dedicating the rest of my life to the memories of my nineteen brothers, but the claims and counterclaims and the legal fights? I wanted no part of that.

CHAPTER THIRTY-ONE

One morning in late July, I stood on the rim of the box canyon in Yarnell. The wind moved fretfully around the ridgeline. Down below, a number of silver foil sheets flashed as the wind blew them here and there, and the saguaro cactus on the next ridge a half mile away appeared to waver in the heat. On the floor of the canyon, the earth was dark, as if it had been singed.

Officials from the Arizona State Forestry Division were moving around on the canyon floor, stopping to take notes or measure a distance. I watched them for a few minutes, then stepped down the gentle gradient. The air cooled as I dropped lower.

To the civilian eye, there was little to look at as I moved across the rough terrain. Some carbonized shrub and that was all; the canyon was moonscaped. When I reached the floor of the shallow canyon, I bent down and touched the char that covered the dirt, as if I were feeling a child's head for fever. Then I began to run my fingers through it.

My hand came up black. Nothing.

I moved to my left, studying the earth and occasionally bending over to scrabble my open palm in a wide arc, feeling the cool ground beneath my skin while the burned material filtered between my fingers. The sun beat down on my back. After a few minutes, my thumb stubbed against something sharp and I drew it back quickly. My hand was bleeding. I ignored it and reached for the thing I had touched: a piece of partially melted glass. I studied it, then I wiped the blood on my pant leg and moved on.

I walked a rough circle encompassing about thirty yards. It was the same area the investigators had concentrated on. By the time the sun was high and the temperature had risen to one hundred degrees, I'd uncovered ten objects, among them a scorched coffee mug, a broken tool head, and a miniature drip torch.

I recognized each of them. Half of the boys had left something behind.

I could picture the events that led these objects to be here. I didn't want to, but the images had been coming to me unbidden for the last month and there was no stopping them.

I looked up at the saddle where Granite Mountain had stood before coming down. What did they see when they peered out at the fire before descending into the canyon? Why did they come down?

I tried to get inside Eric's head. Which way to go, along the two-track road or down into the green box canyon? He saw the fire moving parallel to the crew and thought they had plenty of time to cut through the canyon and make Boulder Springs Ranch. They'd save time. Would he rather be marching for those minutes or fighting the fire, saving homes, maybe saving lives?

We don't know what the canyon floor looked like that day. All we know is the nuked landscape we found after the disaster. How high was the brush? How many twenty-foot trees were in front of them, exactly?

The strong outflow winds that had been predicted fifty minutes before hadn't arrived at 4:15 p.m. Eric scanned the terrain and decided to take a risk, based on years of experience. He brought his men into the canyon.

Then there was a second decision, once they were deep into the chaparral and they could hear the fire approaching from the east. They had three options: head back up the wall of the canyon to the two-track road, deploy where they were, or make a run toward the ranch.

Heading back up the way they came would have been a nonstarter. The slope would have been covered in flames by then. Option number one was out. And the thickness of the chaparral would have made running impossible. Obviously they hadn't spotted the wash that now lay to my left. It was clear as day to me, with the juniper and the pine burned away. But they hadn't seen it from the saddle.

Did the guys think of dropping their packs and running? Did they debate it there on the canyon floor, shouting to each other as the fire drowned out their voices? From the positions their bodies were found in, I know that each of them made the decision to stick with his brothers. No one ran.

Another thing I do know: Eric would never have brought Granite Mountain into the canyon if he thought it presented a real danger to the men. That's nonnegotiable. Eric Marsh didn't take stupid risks.

But he did take risks. We all did. It's intrinsic to the whole idea of hotshottin'. And it's not as if you're taking on these risks to climb Everest or shoot some Class VI rapids in a canoe. You're trying to save something: a house, a forest, a community.

I thought back to that dedication in my firefighting manual I'd first opened when I was fourteen:

> to the members of that unselfish organization of men and women who hold devotion to duty above personal risk, who count on sincerity and service above personal comfort and convenience, who strive unceasingly to find better ways of protecting the lives, homes and property of their fellow citizens from the ravages of fire and other disasters ...
> THE FIREFIGHTERS OF ALL NATIONS.

It didn't say anything about firefighter safety in there. Or about self-preservation. Not that those things weren't taught in my training.

Yes, every hotshot is taught not to go into the green, especially into a box canyon bristling with chaparral, with a flaming front approaching you. That is undeniable. All I can think is that they thought they had the time. And in a normal fire, they would have. But this was far from a normal fire. Thirteen or fifteen miles per hour doesn't sound like much, but if you're moving at five miles per hour and in no way can you go any faster, it's fast as hell.

I looked again at the objects at my feet. The piece of glass had belonged to Jesse, part of a jar filled with coffee that he always carried. The tool head had belonged to Chris. There was part of a mug that Eric had carried with him to every job, and here it was, still intact, though black as pitch.

I closed my eyes. I could see the guys desperately cutting down brush to create a deployment site, heaving away their tools as the fire reached the canyon floor. I knew they were probably gasping for breath, struggling out of their packs to get to the rolled-up fire shelters, all as the wildfire bore down on them from above. Their thoughts quickly grew confused, their brains starved of oxygen. The noise would have been deafening by then. The smoke would have been thick and bristling with cinders, a solid black river eight or ten feet tall, scorching their lungs as they breathed.

Then the superheated air that rushed over them as if a blast furnace door had been thrown open incinerated their special Nomex clothes as they crouched inside the shelters. The objects made of more durable material were freed from their pockets and dropped to the ground. And there they were, all that was left of June 30.

I touched the objects one by one, turning them over in my hands. I took each one and pictured the face of the man it belonged to and held that picture for a moment before relinquishing it. My hands were thick with the black soot that I knew contained trace amounts of the bodies of my friends. It didn't repel me to touch this dust.

I missed the guys so much. I just wanted to be near them. But this would be as close as I could ever get.

I was tempted to slip one or two of the items into my pocket as keepsakes. But the investigators wanted everything connected with the wildfire. They came over, bagged the things up, and stood up. They promised me they'd pass them on to the families. I nodded.

They left me alone.

I was glad I'd come to Yarnell. The last things left by the men were on their way back to their families; perhaps they'd bring them some comfort.

But the questions that had obsessed me since the tragedy,

and which had brought me to the canyon a month after the fire, hadn't gone away:

Why did my brothers die and leave me here? Why didn't they take me with them? Is it possible to continue on without them?

CHAPTER THIRTY-TWO

Three months after the tragedy, I'd lost all semblance of a normal life. I didn't know who I was outside of what had happened at Yarnell. I'd never really grieved for my brothers; I'd become their spokesman, in a way, and I was glad to do it. But I felt like I was losing my mind.

Not having my brothers around was hell. Not having the job came a close second. There's nothing I'd have liked better than to grab my Pulaski and head out with a crew to a hill fire and just work a wildfire, fourteen days straight like we used to. But I couldn't, mostly because of my daughter.

Michaela was still anxious from the days when I'd say good-bye and disappear for two weeks. Any time I got up to go to the grocery store or go to the target range with my compound bow, she'd come running up to me.

"Daddy, no firefighting, right?" Her face scrunched up as her eyes searched mine for an answer.

"No, baby. No firefighting." I got tears in my eyes, but I smiled.

She knew about Yarnell. We'd drive around town and see guys wearing Granite Mountain memorial T-shirts and see cars with stickers on them and she'd get happy. "That's Daddy's work!" She knew about Yarnell, but she didn't understand.

What else was I qualified to do outside of fighting fires? I had few marketable skills, unless you want to call selling pot a marketable skill. Hotshottin' was what made me a father. It was the only thing I had to provide for Michaela. Now the one person I'd do anything for didn't want me to do the one thing I knew how to do and do well. That was a riddle I couldn't solve.

I went to work for the Wildland Firefighter Foundation, which helps the families of fallen and injured hotshots. I spoke with families. I encouraged guys who'd been burned to get help. I enjoyed the work. But, in a way, I was a hypocrite. I was avoiding therapy. I was surrounding myself with people who'd been through similar tragedies, but I wasn't taking my own advice.

I was reliving the tragedy every day in the work I did. But I didn't feel I deserved help. I felt it was only right of me to give and not receive.

The fire affected everyone around me, not just Michaela. My mom had been working as a housesitter for a wealthy family on the outskirts of Prescott. When the fire happened, she heard the choppers coming in. She sat in the empty house and imagined me dying. After Yarnell, she quit that job—working in the house reminded her of how close I'd come to not being here.

She wanted to be happy that I was still around, but she was surrounded by mothers who didn't have their sons. She didn't want to make a big deal about her happiness. She knew the guys, Chris especially. We'd spent Thanksgiving and Christmas together. So she was mourning them at the same time she was trying to celebrate.

It's a strange thing to be a lone survivor. Everyone is happy you made it out, but still, you're a reminder that no one else did.

No one can be completely happy you're still here. Not even your mother.

A year after the tragedy, Natalie moved to Phoenix, so twice a week, I drove to Cordes Junction, which is the halfway point between her place and Prescott. Natalie would be waiting at a gas station we'd chosen and I'd either drop Michaela off or pick her up. On the way there or back, Michaela and I would laugh and talk and scream out her favorite songs when they came on the radio, competing to see who could sing the loudest. I loved those rides, especially when I picked her up. Then I had a week with her to look forward to. Those hours were the center of my life.

But as the weeks went by, I found I was responding less to my daughter. I wasn't as sad when I dropped her off or as happy when I picked her up. I had less emotion, period. I was just drifting, a blank person.

Michaela sensed the change in me. She's a smart kid. She would ask me if anything was wrong, and I saw her eyes searching my face for the old signs of silliness. I tried to sing her songs, but my voice sounded fake. I couldn't even manufacture enough emotion to fool a three-year-old. I felt like a robot whose battery was running down.

One Monday in the summer of 2014, Michaela and I were driving to the halfway point and I was telling Michaela how much I loved her. She nodded, tapping her foot to the music. I could hear my voice go on and on. Flatlined. The emotion seemed to have drained out a hole in the bottom of my heart.

While she looked at the passing cars out the passenger window, I cried, knowing I wouldn't see her for another week.

We reached Cordes Junction and I spotted Natalie. Michaela was trying to see over the seat to get a glimpse of her mom, super excited. I parked the truck, got out, went around, and opened Michaela's door. I undid her seat belt and picked her up. As I was setting her on the ground, she wriggled free and ran off to jump into her mother's arms. She was laughing and yelling.

She can't wait to get away from you, I thought.

That hit me hard. I could see that Michaela lit up when she saw her mom, and it was only then that I realized how much my depression was affecting her. *It's a relief to get away from you.* And that thought was a killer.

Years ago, before Granite Mountain, I'd said to myself, *Get sober for Michaela or kill yourself.* I'd gotten sober, but now I was holding her back again. I was a negative force in her life. I was hurting her just by being around.

I got back in the truck. I started it up and turned around, got on Route 17 back toward Prescott.

It's time to go, I thought. *You're making Michaela sad. You might be damaging her for life. You're a failure as a dad.*

A little more than halfway home, I pulled over to the side of the road, the tires slipping and grinding on the gravel there. I sat for a moment with the motor running, the radio playing some commercial for an auto dealer. Then I reached into my glove compartment and pulled out my nine-millimeter.

I had only one thought in my head: *I can't do this anymore.* I was so empty. There was no hope for me. It was as if I could see my life stretching out for the next fifty years and every single day looked the same: depressed, hopeless.

And each day I would rob a little more color out of my daughter's life.

The PTSD was only going to get worse. The nightmares were only going to get worse. The depression would deepen.

I laid the gun on the passenger seat. All that lay between me and my brothers was five pounds of trigger pull. Cars and trucks were shooting by on my left, people in the windows on their way to whatever. Jobs, kids, homes. I felt so separated from them.

I should have done more at Yarnell, I thought. Tears were stinging my eyes. *I could have done something. I'm responsible for Yarnell. How exactly, I'm not sure, but I could have saved those guys. What does a lookout do? He* looks out for his friends. *Fucking simple enough. So why didn't I do it?*

Memories of the fire came back to me in vivid detail. I heard a Granite Mountain crew member's last call on the radio. "Air Attack, Granite Mountain Seven!" in that horrible, anguished voice. Then the noises of the saws in the background, the sirens, the smells, the rush to the hills, the body bags, the funerals. It was a flood of images and sensations.

I reached down and picked up the gun in my right hand.

I felt the weight of the thing in my hand. *Just put it to your temple and get it over with. Go be with your friends. Best thing for everyone.*

There was another memory flickering in my head: me and Michaela two hours before, in my house, dancing to a song on the radio. I thought about that for a minute.

The cars droned by. I thought of the guys who would find me with my brains splattered all over the truck window. The word getting to my relatives and friends. The looks of shock and grief on their faces. Then the families of the nineteen, going through it all over again. More horrible shit all around.

I thought about Michaela growing up thinking her dad hadn't fought hard enough to stay with her.

I felt as if there was a balance in my head with one side weighed down with reasons to live and the other with reasons to die. That little sliver of a thought seemed to tip the scales. I didn't want to be a coward in my daughter's memory. I very much wanted to kill myself at that moment. But the cost for everyone else would just be too high.

There was no rush of happiness. Reluctantly, I racked my gun and the bullet from the chamber popped out and landed on the passenger seat. I pulled out the magazine and threw it and the gun into the backseat. I put the truck in gear and spun the tires in the gravel as I accelerated back onto the highway.

I needed help. But I still wouldn't go to therapy. Too stubborn. Too afraid to admit I needed help.

Soon after that incident, in the fall of 2014, more than a year after the tragedy, I traveled to two memorials for the Granite Mountain Hotshots. After the first one was over, the thoughts of suicide returned. The second one was at the National Fallen Firefighters Memorial. After it was over, a bunch of the firefighters and their families went to a local bar to talk and reminisce. At one point, I was standing alone, a beer in my hand, pain churning in my heart.

A woman came up to me, a therapist from Phoenix that I'd met earlier. Her name was Kerry. She had a calmness about her. I was anything but calm.

"So how are you doing, Brendan?"

Such a simple question. I looked at her.

"You really want to know?"

"Yes, I do."

"I feel like shit. I feel like this is never going to end."

She nodded. The words began to pour out of me: how I felt trapped in an endless cycle of guilt, anger, sorrow, and disgust that I was still alive. The memorials just brought it all back.

I must have talked for half an hour, and the woman just nodded and held my gaze.

Within a week, I was in counseling with a therapist Kerry found for me in Prescott. It saved my life.

CHAPTER THIRTY-THREE

In the beginning, the therapy didn't work. In fact, it made things worse.

The type of counseling I was in is called EMDR, or eye movement desensitization and reprocessing. It sounds bizarre: You relive the memories that have affected you while doing some other motion, like moving your eyes left and right. It was developed to battle PTSD.

What was amazing to me was that I thought I was going to work on my feelings about Yarnell and life, but in my first sessions I discovered I had no feelings left. Only a wall of depression. In order to stop experiencing those black moods, I'd blocked off all emotions. It took me three sessions simply to open up and allow myself to experience real feelings again.

I began by describing to the therapist a "point of disturbance," a memory that has haunted me. We started with the time Chris and I almost got burned a couple of weeks before Yarnell. I would do the eye motions as I relived those things I had buried deep down.

It was so hurtful to go through it all again. I sat in that

darkened room and talked with my counselor and I honestly felt like my skin had been peeled off and salt water was pouring over me. Everything was so raw. I would cry and shake my head.

We'd go through the experience from beginning to end, and then the therapist would ask me how I felt about what I'd just described. I had to dig for every negative emotion connected with that time: the guilt I felt, the anger I never knew I had toward myself or someone else. Dredge it up. And then she'd ask commonsense questions about whether those emotions were really based in reality. What was I supposed to do from the lookout position to save my brothers? And slowly, she would show me the positive side of what I'd gone through: that I'd persevered. That I'd done my best. That I'd kept faith with my brothers.

I had a lot to learn about myself. I found out so many things about my childhood. I learned that I'd felt abandoned throughout my life: by my father, my brother, even my mom. Then to have my nineteen brothers disappear on that hillside? It only compounded that feeling: *Everyone you love is going to leave you.* That abandonment was really at the root of my depression. I felt that there was something wrong with me, because no one wanted to stay by my side.

That's why Eric's acceptance of me had been such a big deal in my life. He looked at me at my lowest point and said, "We'll take you, brother." The other guys had reinforced that feeling again and again: "You're a good father. You're worth something. We trust you. We love you."

When I lost that, I found it hard to live.

I remember the session where that fact came home to me. I walked out feeling drained and listless, as usual. But later that day, I suddenly realized that the lead weight that had been sitting on top of me seemed lighter. It wasn't gone, but I could bear it. I'd turned that experience around in my mind and looked at it from a different angle.

I had honestly thought I was serving a life sentence. I didn't think it was even possible to feel differently about my past. But it is possible. If you've gone through something that left you with PTSD, I want you to know that. You can get free of the things that are weighing you down and slowly killing the joy in your life. There is hope. You just have to reach out for it.

My life improved bit by bit. My emotions came back. Michaela and I were able to be two silly kids again without me feeling like I was damaging her. In the course of a day, I felt happy and sad and pissed off and contented. Normal feelings.

I came to terms with the fact that I had PTSD. I learned that the thing that kills men is the idea that they need to be tough. Everyone tells you to get help, but as a man you believe you should be giving help, not receiving it. And that's the crucial mistake. If you say "I can get through anything alone," you're suffering for no reason.

Accept help. Be open. Find what's worked for others and do that.

One of the breakthrough moments came when I thought of the family members who'd accused me of awful things. The bitterness I'd felt was suddenly gone. They'd suffered. They, too, wanted answers to why their loved ones had left them, and I was available as a bad guy or a conspirator or what have you. I understood that their wild accusations were part of their grieving process.

I don't hold anything against them now. I love them to

death. Do I wish they never said those kinds of things? Sure. But at three a.m., when you're all alone, crazy thoughts can come into your mind. The pain is unbearable. You find a villain and that gives you a moment's relief. In their situation, I'm sure I would have done the same thing.

CHAPTER THIRTY-FOUR

Even though I made progress, there were things that triggered the bad old thoughts. Even now, every time we get to March and April, I can feel myself tensing up. Fire season is starting again. Despite all the investigations and reports on Yarnell, nothing's really changed on the ground for hotshots. It's still the same tools, the same procedures, the same fire conditions, if not worse. I dread waking up one day and hearing on the news that a crew got trapped in a wildfire and a bunch of guys died.

It's inevitable. Someone has to fight the flames and fire is an unpredictable and dangerous thing. But I wish there was a better way.

I wanted to change things. *How can we make it safer out there?* I got a call the other day from someone working on a new fire shelter. The old ones, the ones used in Yarnell, can withstand up to maybe 700 degrees of radiant heat. The guys working on this new one want a shelter that can take up to 1,700 degrees.

That's great. That would be a big plus for hotshots. But every solution seems to have a hidden black lining.

History has shown us that the better the equipment you give firefighters, the deeper into the fire they're going to want to push. They'll use the better equipment to become more effective firefighters. It's a catch-22: Give a man a bulletproof vest, and he'll get that much closer to his adversary.

But there are things we can do to make all wildland firefighters safer. The first is a tracking system for each firefighter. Right now hotshots have GPS on them and can report in where they are by radio. But in extreme conditions, when the fire is bearing down on you, you're not thinking about giving your position. You're thinking about living for the next 120 seconds. Communications during a fire can be sketchy. The saw is buzzing in your ears and the fire is ripping up a stand of trees; it's loud out there. Sometimes guys just don't hear the radio. And sometimes it's hard to hear what someone in the field is trying to tell you.

So we need a locator that can transmit the hotshot's position continuously and that everyone in the field can see in real time. A supervisor sitting in a truck somewhere would have a computer on his lap with the up-to-the-second location of every hotshot. With eyes on the fire, he could tell them what's coming at them. *The fire is shifting your way. Get out.*

These locators exist. They're called SENDs, or satellite emergency notification devices, and they look like small walkie-talkies that can fit in the palm of your hand. They often work off satellite signals when there is no cell service available, and they function even in the 20 percent of forest terrain that cannot get radio coverage, so they're perfect for fighting fires in the wilderness. In April 2012, more than a year before Yarnell, the U.S. Forest Service notified tech companies that it was in the market to buy such a device. They ended up purchasing thousands of them, but Granite Mountain didn't have them at Yarnell.

Every hotshot in America should have one.

A SEND also contains an SOS button. The firefighter hits it and the dispatchers monitoring the system instantly know two things: that the hotshot is in trouble, and his or her exact location. That alert also warns fellow hotshots that there's something really dangerous at the exact spot their buddy is working.

A helicopter pilot bringing in a load of water would be able to spot a trapped crew and dump right over them. Other hotshots could roll toward them on their UTVs. It would be a complete, coordinated response, and it would be fast.

A system like that might have helped at Yarnell. The pilot in that VLAT that was hovering above the ridge would have known instantaneously that the crew was in trouble and their exact position. Could he have laid a line of retardant across them? He would have had only one shot at it. Maybe he'd make it. Maybe not. But it was more of a chance than they had.

The tech part is easier than the philosophy. A lot of people think hotshots need to increase their margin of safety, get farther away from the burning edge. That's a tough one. There's a basic conflict between the effectiveness of a hotshot crew and their safety. How are you going to tell a crew, "There are people's houses over the next ridge that are under threat, but we're holding you here"? What's the point of having firefighters in the field, then? It's like telling marines, "A village is being burned to the ground, but it's too dangerous to send you in." The last person who wants to hear that kind of thing is a hotshot.

One thing I do know: More helicopters, more firefighters, and more tanker planes would help. The more resources you put into a wildfire, the safer it is for everyone. But either the money isn't there for new tankers or it's not going to the places it needs to go.

I don't blame people who want their houses saved. But some people don't want to pay the extra taxes to see that we have everything we need. An on-call tanker costs around $14,000 a day. Put it in the air, and the bill soars to $4,200 an hour. Big helicopters are even more expensive: upward of $30,000 a day for on-call duty, and over $6,000 an hour for in-flight.

Add in millions for a new tanker when the fire is gone? Nine times out of ten, the answer is no.

Two years after Yarnell, I was listening to the news when I heard about a wildfire in Washington. Four firefighters had been trying to get away from the flames and had crashed their truck. The fire caught them and three perished with one survivor who sustained major burn injuries.

I sat down and cried and cried. I felt sick. It was happening again. The same elements as Yarnell: Dry tinder. Fast-moving winds. A red flag warning in the area. A change in direction in the fire wall. And firefighters trying to do their job, dying. I thought of their families, especially, the years of searing pain that lie ahead of them.

Something has to change. *Has to*.

We need a wildland firefighters union in America. It's beyond clear to me that these men and women are continuously being put into dangerous situations where they have no voice and no power. It's time for a union that will fight for what wildland firefighters need in order to do their job. Better pay. Better working conditions. More resources. And, most important of all, improved safety.

When your house catches on fire, the men and women who show up to help you belong to a union. The International Association of Fire Fighters has a quarter million members, and they all have fairer pay and better working conditions than almost any wildland firefighter in America. That's just wrong.

Wildfires are getting bigger. They're burning hotter, wider, and longer. As I write this, twenty thousand firefighters are in the field in the West—and it's not enough. The government is giving National Guard troops emergency wildfire training so they can help out crews that are stretched beyond their limits. There's a crew of twenty firefighters working a thirty-two-hour shift on a fire line somewhere in California. They're bone tired. They haven't seen their families in weeks. They're working under supervisors who are exhausted and overworked. When that crew kills the fire they're on, there are two or three more waiting for them. It's inevitable that mistakes will be made.

Sadly, 2015 was a horrible year for wildfires. More are coming.

I'll be the first to admit I'm not an expert. I'm not a veteran hotshot; I was a seasonal employee who saw a lot of action during a time of drought. But three seasons was enough to at least show that there was a problem in how we fight wildfires nationally. One headline from Washington is enough, if it talks about fatalities. Innovation in how we fight wildfires needs to start somewhere. If I can help spark that change, I'd feel what I've gone through had some meaning beyond me.

When I go around the country talking about this book, I'm going to meet with firefighters. I'm going to ask them about their lives and talk about the future of our profession. Firefighters have insights that the people making decisions about our lives don't have. We know what works and what doesn't. We can be a force for good. Maybe joining together is the way to get there.

The system we have isn't working, period. Guys are dying in the same exact scenarios that were killing hotshots fifty or seventy-five years ago. The *exact* same scenarios. These hardworking men and women need to come home at night to the people who love them.

EPILOGUE

The Pioneers' Home Cemetery sits high on a hill in Prescott. It was once the site of a retirement home for the early settlers, gunfighters, saloon piano players, and miners who came to Arizona in the 1800s during its blood-and-thunder days and built the state. Many of those pioneers are buried in plots that dot the hilltop overlooking the city. In a separate section, gathered into a memorial made of granite and bronze, are the graves of my brothers, the Yarnell nineteen.

I go there when I can. Not too often, to be honest. It's painful, still, more than I can describe. What happens when I first walk up to the bronze memorial plaques laid out in a rectangle is that I remember the rain we had the day we dedicated the memorial. And then I see the faces of the families from the funerals. I went to each funeral, and I remember each one vividly.

I just walk around the memorial and let the memories come. I couldn't stop them if I tried. I can't stop the pain I feel. I just let it happen. Aunts, mothers, fathers, daughters: I see all their faces and it's like I can hear them crying all over again.

But I love this place, in a way. I've told my family I want to be buried here. That was an easy call. Many of the loved ones of the guys have said the same thing: They want to lie next to their son when the time comes. I want to be with my brothers. That's where home has been for me ever since I met them. I want my grandkids to come visit and see my name and then read about the other guys and hear stories about what kind of men they were. There are stone benches for them to sit on. That gives me comfort, imagining my grandson sitting there and my daughter telling him what his grandpa did and how the other men gave their lives for their work and each other. There's no point in remembering me without remembering Eric and Jesse and Chris and Travis and the rest of the boys, because without them I would have been a different man, a far less honorable person.

Is it strange, at twenty-three years old, to think about my burial plot? Not for me. It's the continuation of what I feel now. I think about the guys every day; I talk to them. There's not a day goes by that I don't encounter a situation where a lesson one of the Granite Mountain guys taught me comes to mind. It could be how to treat every moment with Michaela like it could be my last. It could be about trying to be honest and fair with everyone I meet. Or giving people a chance, like Eric did for me.

Do I always live up to their memories? Hell no. I mess up all the time. But I never even had that ideal to try to reach before. Now I do. Those guys are with me as much as my daughter or my mother is, and so I look forward to being alongside them for good.

Therapy has gotten me here, talking through that day at Yarnell and untangling the emotions that come with it. I'll never lose the horrible memories I have, but I can change the way I feel about them. The counseling I've had isn't like surgery; it doesn't remove the pain the way a surgeon removes a cancerous tumor. I've accepted that I'll always have flashbacks to June 30, 2013. The memorials, the faces, the crinkly feel of those orange body bags, they're part of me.

But I've been allowed to grieve these men now. I've accepted that I couldn't have saved them, no matter what I did. For so long, I felt that Eric and the others gave me so much that I owed them something in their final moments, that I needed to save them the way they saved me, and I didn't do that. And that's what hurt me the most.

But that's not what happened. What happened was a wildfire that ran out of control. I didn't fail my brothers, and they didn't abandon me.

The people who chose the location for the Pioneers' Home Cemetery knew what they were doing. It's a peaceful place. The wind blows across the hilltop and all you can hear is the leaves fluttering in the trees and the flags snapping on their poles. It's just the blue sky and the granite and the faces etched into the bronze. You're alone up there, but you're not alone.

Before I leave, I give one last look to the bronze plates, see what the families or strangers have left. Stuffed toys. Little bottles of whiskey or bourbon, in memory of a night with one of the guys years ago, most likely. Sometimes veterans leave the medals they earned overseas. Firefighters from all over the country leave their patches in remembrance. It would surprise you how many Americans still have the guys close to their hearts.

When I'm up there, I do feel that my brothers are at

peace. There are even times I envy them that. I'm not at peace yet. But it will come one day, that I know.

After an hour or so at Pioneers' Home, I get in my pickup truck and drive. I let the memories fade away for the moment and I head home and pick up Michaela, tell her about my day. Only by learning to live with what happened at Yarnell, and accepting the gift that my brothers gave me, can I be with the people I love.

I understand that now. It was a hard lesson to learn.

ACKNOWLEDGMENTS

I want to thank God for blessing me with the strength and courage to endure and the compassion to move forward. I want to thank my mother for always being there for me through thick and thin and standing behind me wholeheartedly during this tragedy.

My girlfriend, Ali, was by my side through all of my depression, anxiety, nightmares, and battle with PTSD. Kevin, Kody, Seth, Wilbur, Michael, Mitch, and Bryan, all of you, thank you for being a shoulder to lean on and a rock to keep me stable.

There are so many others: The families of my brothers have given me amazing support and have stood with me since the beginning; your approval has meant the world to me. The counselors who showed me there was hope when I was hopeless. My newfound family and friends who helped guide me through this tragedy and donated so much more than just money to assist my brothers' families and me. The nonprofits that helped those of us in the deepest pain. The public service men and women who made my brothers' memorials and funerals everything we could have asked for. My brothers out there on the fire line, who kick ass and save lives time and time again. The community and nation that made sure my brothers are remembered as heroes—and who refuse to forget those men and women who serve every day.

My deepest thanks to my brothers. The lessons and sacrifices you made will never be forgotten. May I continue to carry on your legacy, though I know my time is borrowed and short.

Most important, thank you to my daughter, Michaela. You're not old enough to read this, but one day you will and you will know what a true angel you have been for your daddy since the day you were born. You continue to keep my feet firmly planted and remind me what God has in store for me.